Soups

100 recipes from classic to contemporary

Bettina Jenkins

APPLE

A LANSDOWNE BOOK

Published by Apple Press in 2005
Sheridan House
4th Floor
112-116 Western Road
Hove
East Sussex BN3 1DD UK

www.apple-press.com

Created and produced by Lansdowne Publishing
Author: Bettina Jenkins
Additional recipe text: Myles Beaufort, Katherine Blakemore, Robert Carmack, Soon Young Chung, Didier Corlou, Shunsuke Fukushima, Nicole Gaunt, Sally Hurworth, Ajoy Joshi, Vicky Liley, Tess Mallos, Sompon Nabnian, Lee Gold, Margaret O'Sullivan, Jan Purser, Lynelle Scott-Aiken, Suzie Smith, Kirsten Tilgals, Brigid Treloar, Nguyen Thanh Van, Linda Venturoni-Wilson, Rosemary Wadey
Commissioned by: Deborah Nixon
Copy Editor: Sarah Shrubb
Photography: Quentin Bacon, Alan Benson, Ben Dearnley, Andrew Elton, Rowan Fotheringham, John Hollingshead, Chris Jones, Vicki Liley, Louise Lister, André Martin, Amanda McLauchlan
Designer: Avril Makula
Production: Sally Stokes, Eleanor Cant
Project Co-ordinator: Sally Hurworth

ISBN 1 84543 052 2

Set in Helvetica on QuarkXPress
Printed in Singapore by Tien Wah Press Pte Ltd

Cover picture: Beef with coconut milk and Thai herbs, see page 60
Pictured on back cover (left to right): Classic beef pho (see page 50), Salmon rice soup (see page 72), Pea and lettuce soup (see page 27)
Pictured on page 2: Potato and cauliflower soup, see page 30

Contents

8   Introduction

10   Basic stocks

16   Creamy soups

32   Chicken and duck

50   Beef and pork

72   Seafood

98   Vegetable

132   Chilled soups

138   Glossary

142   Index

Recipes

Basic stocks

Chicken stock

Beef stock

Vegetable stock

Fish stock

Hot and sour stock

Laksa paste

Basic miso soup

Creamy soups

Curried parsnip soup with
parsnip chips

Spicy squash and bean soup

Creamy beet and potato borscht

Potato and watercress soup

Creamed squash and potato soup

Cream of tomato soup

Curried split pea soup

Creamy squash and leek soup

Steamed squash soup with
hazelnuts

Cream of spinach soup

Pea and lettuce soup

Caldo verde (Spinach soup)

Cream of broccoli soup

Du Barry soup

Potato and cauliflower soup

Chicken and duck

Chicken laksa

Chicken and mushroom soup

Sweet potato chowder with chicken

Chicken and coconut milk soup

Chicken vermicelli soup with egg

Chicken and sweet corn soup

Vietnamese chicken and rice soup

Chicken soup

Hot and sour chicken soup

Chicken and noodle soup

Ramen noodle and roast duck soup

Roast duck and sweet potato soup

Beef and pork

Classic beef pho

Quick beef and pepper soup

Meatball soup

Borscht

Beef and barley soup

Beef and cabbage soup

Beef soup with ginger and
asparagus

Marinated beef laksa

Beef with coconut milk and
Thai herbs

Hearty potato and salami soup

Spicy corn and tomato soup
with chorizo

Split pea and ham soup

Smoked ham minestrone

Red lentil, potato and ham soup

Udon noodle soup with sesame
pork and mushroom

Pork wonton, asparagus and
noodle soup

Somen noodle, pork and
scallion soup

Seafood

Salmon rice soup

Hot and sour soup with shrimp

Shrimp bisque

Shrimp and onion soup

Shrimp, tomato and chili soup

Indian fish soup

Mussels in spiced coconut milk
  broth

Bouillabaise

Seafood soup

Clam chowder

Fennel and oyster soup

Scallop and potato soup

Scallop and leek soup

Poached salmon and
  green bean soup

Crab and asparagus soup

Sour crabmeat soup

Coconut-shrimp soup

Seafood laksa

Miso with tuna and ginger

Marinated shrimp, noodle and
  herb soup

Marinated lime-and-chili fish soup

Vegetable

Tofu and vegetable soup

Pea, potato, leek and tofu soup

Sweet potato, chili and coconut
  soup

Spicy tomato and cauliflower soup

Curried cauliflower soup

Chunky vegetable soup

Peasant bean soup

Country vegetable soup with pasta

Tomato soup

Spinach and lentil soup

Vegetable and lentil soup

Vichyssoise with Thai herbs

Carrot and ginger soup

Rustic potato soup with Thai spices

French onion soup

Mushroom-barley soup

Mushroom and cilantro soup

Mushroom soup

Red lentil soup

Japanese watercress

Corn, squash, rice and spinach
  soup

Chili-corn soup

Vegetable minestrone

Sweet potato, carrot, ginger and
  tofu soup

Carrot soup with Asian greens and
  coconut

Mushroom wonton, noodle and
  spinach soup

Butternut squash and coconut
  milk soup

Chinese noodle soup

Vegetable and rice noodle soup
  (Buddha's delight)

Coconut and vegetable soup

Vegetable pho

Chilled soups

Gazpacho

Cold apricot and pear soup

Cold avocado soup

Asparagus and dill soup

Chilled cucumber and ginger soup

Roasted red bell pepper soup

Vichyssoise

Introduction

Soups are versatile, simple to prepare and tasty. Most ingredients can be transformed into soups, and their endless varieties mean they can be served as starters, main meals or as a quick snack. They can be served hot and hearty or cold and smooth. There is sure to be a soup to satisfy everyone.

Soup is a liquid food which is simply made by simmering various ingredients, including meat, fish, vegetables and herbs. Soup can then be transformed by the addition of rice, pasta, noodles and a variety of other ingredients.

The liquid in which most soups are cooked is stock, and the success of a soup begins with this versatile ingredient. Stock is used instead of water in many dishes, particularly soups, to enhance their flavor. A well flavored stock will produce a well flavored soup. Although ready made stocks and stock cubes are readily available and are a great time saver, the flavor doesn't compare to the real thing! Home made stocks are extremely simple and economical to prepare—they will keep in the refrigerator for 2–3 days or can be successfully frozen for later use.

Soups come in a variety of forms. Some are based on stock – these are amongst the simplest to prepare. They are wholesome soups, not delicate, and require hearty ingredients like legumes, pasta, rice and potatoes to bulk them up. Minestrone and Chunky Vegetable Soup are examples.

Pureed soups, like Cream of Tomato Soup, Vichyssoise and Cream of Spinach Soup, are smooth soups which have been pureed after thorough cooking. The consistency of a pureed soup will vary according to the ingredients used and the pureeing method.

Cream soups are pureed soups which have been enriched with cream or yogurt, or they are soups which are thickened with a roux (flour and butter). They are richer and smoother than pureed soups.

Fish and shellfish soups include famous soups like Bouillabaise and Clam Chowder. These are both hearty soups, chowder being stew like. Bisques are a rich smooth soup, usually made from shellfish.

Other soups are served chilled, like the famous Gazpacho, often described as soup-salad and served icy cold. Ideal for picnics and outdoor entertaining, chilled soups make a refreshing addition to a summer menu.

Soups can be served quite simply, or enhanced by the addition of garnishes. These are many and varied and can include crispy croutons, fresh herbs, yogurt, crème fraîche or crusty bread. Garnishes can transform a soup—a simple swirl of cream, a dollop of pesto, some fried bacon or a fine julienne of vegetables—and add extra flavor, color and texture. No matter how you serve soup, you will feel good knowing that you have served a tasty meal that will satisfy most taste buds.

RIGHT Vegetable pho, page 131

Basic stocks

Chicken stock

1 whole chicken, about 2 lb (1 kg)
1 large onion, roughly sliced
1 large carrot, roughly chopped
2 sticks celery, chopped
5 cilantro (fresh coriander) stems, including roots
1 teaspoon sea salt
8 black peppercorns
10 cups (80 fl oz/2.5 L) cold water

Place chicken, onion, carrot, celery, cilantro, salt and peppercorns in a large saucepan and add enough water to cover completely, approximately 10 cups (80 fl oz/2.5 L). Place over medium–high heat and bring liquid to a boil.

Reduce heat to medium–low and simmer for 1–1½ hours, skimming surface occasionally to remove scum and fat.

Remove saucepan from heat. Remove chicken and strain liquid. Allow stock to cool completely, then remove remaining fat from surface.

Stock can be refrigerated (cover tightly with plastic wrap first) for up to 3 days or frozen for up to 3 months.
Makes 8 cups (64 fl oz/2 L)

Beef stock

10 lb (5 kg) beef bones
1 teaspoon sea salt
3 medium yellow (brown) onions, roughly sliced
2 carrots, roughly chopped
2 sticks celery, with leaves, roughly chopped
1 teaspoon black peppercorns

Preheat oven to 400°F (200°C/Gas 6). Place beef bones in a large baking pan and brush lightly with oil. Bake, turning once, until golden brown all over, about 40 minutes.

Transfer beef bones to a large stockpot and add enough water to cover. Place over high heat and bring to a boil. Boil for 2 minutes. Strain liquid through a large sieve or colander. Discard liquid and keep bones.

Return bones to the stockpot. Add sea salt and enough water to cover bones completely, approximately 10 cups (80 fl oz/2.5 L). Bring to a boil over high heat. Reduce heat to medium–low, add remaining ingredients and simmer for 3–4 hours. Strain stock, discard solids and skim off any residue.

Let stock cool, then cover with plastic wrap and refrigerate if not using immediately. Stock can be refrigerated for up to 4 days or frozen for up to 1 month.
Makes 8 cups (64 fl oz/2 L)

Hint

For beef pho stock, add 1 x 2 in (5 cm) piece fresh ginger, 2 toasted star anise, 1 cinnamon stick, 5 cardamom pods and 2 tablespoons fish sauce to the simmering stock.

Vegetable stock

2 onions, roughly sliced
2 large carrots, roughly chopped
2 sticks celery, roughly chopped
2 leeks, roughly sliced
4 oz (125 g) mushrooms, sliced
1–2 cloves garlic
handful of fresh parsley, stems included
1 teaspoon sea salt or to taste
8 black peppercorns
10 cups (80 fl oz/2.5 L) water

Place onion, carrot, celery, leeks, mushrooms, garlic, parsley, salt and peppercorns in a large saucepan and add 10 cups (80 fl oz/2.5 L) cold water to cover. Place over medium–high heat and bring liquid to a boil. Reduce heat to medium–low and simmer for 1–1½ hours, skimming surface occasionally to remove scum and fat.

Remove saucepan from heat. Strain liquid, but use the back of a large spoon to press vegetables into the strainer – this will enhance the flavor. Stock can be refrigerated for 2–3 days or frozen for up to 3 months.
Makes 8 cups (64 fl oz/2 L)

Hint

For maximum flavor, lightly broil (grill) or roast the vegetables before making the stock. Leaving the vegetable skins on also improves the flavor and color of the stock.

Fish stock

about 2 lb (1 kg) heads and bones of 2 medium-sized
  white-fleshed fish
2 tablespoons light olive oil
1 large onion, roughly chopped
1 large carrot, peeled and roughly chopped
2 stalk celery, with leaves, roughly chopped
3 stems flat-leaf (Italian) parsley
3 stems cilantro (fresh coriander), including roots
3 fresh or 6 dried kaffir lime leaves (optional)
8 black peppercorns
1 teaspoon sea salt

Wash fish heads and bones well, removing any gills.
Chop bones to fit into a large pot.

Heat oil in a large pot over high heat for 1 minute.
Add fish heads and bones and cook, stirring and turning
heads and bones, until any remaining flesh starts to
cook and is slightly golden, 4–5 minutes.

Add remaining ingredients and stir to combine. Add
enough water to cover bones completely (approximately
8 cups/64 fl oz/2 L), and bring liquid to a steady simmer.
Reduce heat to medium and simmer for 25 minutes.
Skim any scum from surface as stock simmers.

Strain liquid through a very fine sieve. If you do not
have a very fine sieve, line your sieve with a double layer
of damp cheesecloth (muslin). Discard solids.

Let stock cool, then cover with plastic wrap and
refrigerate if not using immediately. Stock can be
refrigerated for 2 days or frozen for 2 months.
Makes 8 cups (64 fl oz/2 L)

Variation: Quick seafood stock

In a stockpot, combine shells of shrimp (prawns), crab or
other crustaceans with weak chicken stock or water.
If desired, add 1–2 onions or white portion of 1–2 leeks,
some celery leaves, 2 carrots, ½ teaspoon whole
peppercorns and salt to taste. Alternatively, the cooking
liquid from raw crab in its shell makes a delicious and
simple seafood stock.

Hot and sour stock

2 tablespoons vegetable oil

1 teaspoon chili powder

2 tablespoons dried shrimp (prawns)

1 stalk lemongrass, bottom 3 in (7.5 cm) only,
   chopped

1 clove garlic, chopped

4 black peppercorns

1 teaspoon galangal powder or 1 tablespoon
   chopped fresh galangal

1 red chili pepper

1 green chili pepper

3 fresh or 6 dried kaffir lime leaves

2 tablespoons fish sauce

2 tablespoons lime juice

½ teaspoon shrimp paste

2 teaspoons finely grated lime zest

8 cups (64 fl oz/2 L) chicken stock (see page 10)

Heat vegetable oil in a large saucepan over medium
heat until hot, about 1 minute. Add chili powder and stir
until oil becomes red, 3–4 minutes. Set aside.

   Place dried shrimp in a food processor and process
until fine, 2–3 minutes. Add remaining ingredients,
except chicken stock, and process to a smooth paste,
about 3 minutes. Return chili oil to heat and add paste.
Cook, stirring, until oil comes to surface, 3–4 minutes.
Add chicken stock and bring mixture to a steady
simmer. Simmer for 15 minutes. Strain mixture through a
fine sieve and set aside. Discard solids.

Makes 8 cups (64 fl oz/2 L)

Laksa paste

¾ cup (4 oz/125 g) dried shrimp (prawns)

12 dried red chili peppers

6–8 scallions (shallots/spring onions), about
   6½ oz (200 g), roughly chopped

6 cloves garlic

1 x 4 in (10 cm) piece fresh ginger, peeled and
   roughly chopped

2 teaspoons dried shrimp paste

2 stalks lemongrass, bottom 3 in (7.5 cm) only,
   chopped

½ cup (3 oz/90 g) candlenuts or blanched almonds

1 tablespoon ground turmeric

½ cup (4 fl oz/125 ml) light olive oil

Place shrimp and chili peppers in a bowl and add
enough boiling water to cover. Allow to stand for
15 minutes. Drain, then place shrimp and chili pepper
mixture in a food processor with remaining ingredients.
Process mixture to a fine paste, 2–3 minutes.

   Transfer paste to a bowl or sterilized jar. Cover tightly
with plastic wrap and keep refrigerated for up to
10 days.

**Makes 1½ cups (12 oz/375 g) (enough for 3 laksa
recipes, each serving 4)**

Basic miso soup

4 cups (32 fl oz/1 L) water
¼ cup (2 fl oz/60 ml) shiromiso (white miso) paste
½ teaspoon instant dashi, or to taste
cubed silken tofu, as desired
2 scallions (shallots/spring onions), thinly sliced
1 tablespoon wakame seaweed, soaked for 2 minutes
   in warm water

Place water in a saucepan and bring to a boil. Place miso paste in a small strainer, holding it over saucepan, and press miso through a strainer with the back of a wooden spoon. Discard any grainy miso left in the strainer. Return soup to a boil and add dashi.

   Divide tofu, scallions and seaweed among individual serving bowls. Pour soup liquid into each bowl and serve immediately.
Serves 4

Hint

Miso is a traditional soup that can be served as an accompaniment to any Japanese meal. It is usually enjoyed as part of a traditional Japanese breakfast. Other ingredients can be added to the soup. Cooked meat, seafood or vegetables such as clams, lobster, pork, daikon, onion, eggplant (aubergine) and enoki mushrooms can be added to individual bowls just before filling with soup and serving.

Note

Shiromiso (white miso) paste is available from Asian food stores. It is pale yellow in color and has a sweet flavor. Miso paste keeps in the refrigerator for up to 1 year.

Creamy soups

Curried parsnip soup with parsnip chips

¼ cup (2 fl oz/60 ml) vegetable oil

1 large onion, chopped

2 cloves garlic, crushed

1 teaspoon ground turmeric

½ teaspoon ground cumin

½ teaspoon ground ginger

½ small chili pepper, seeded and sliced

1¼ lb (625 g) parsnips, peeled and chopped

2 cooking apples, peeled, cored and chopped

4 cups (32 fl oz/1 L) vegetable stock (see page 11)

salt and freshly ground black pepper, to taste

1 cup (8 fl oz/250 ml) light (single) cream

FOR PARSNIP CHIPS

4 parsnips, peeled

3 cups (24 fl oz/750 ml) vegetable oil, for deep-frying

To make parsnip chips: Thinly slice each parsnip lengthwise with a vegetable peeler. Heat oil in a large, deep, heavy-bottomed saucepan or deep-fat fryer until it reaches 375°F (190°C) on a deep-frying thermometer or until a small cube of bread dropped into the oil sizzles and turns golden. Working in handfuls, add parsnip slices to hot oil and deep-fry until golden, about 1 minute. Using a slotted spoon, remove chips from oil and drain on paper towels.

Warm oil in a large saucepan over medium heat. Add onion and garlic and cook until onion softens, about 2 minutes. Stir in turmeric, cumin, ginger and chili pepper, and cook for 3 minutes, stirring occasionally. Add parsnips and apples and stir well. Cover and cook for 5 minutes, stirring occasionally. Stir in vegetable stock and season with salt and pepper. Bring mixture to a boil over high heat, then reduce heat to a simmer. Cover and simmer until parsnips are soft, about 30–40 minutes.

Remove soup from heat and transfer to a large bowl. Working in batches, ladle into a food processor and process until smooth, about 20 seconds. Return soup to the saucepan and heat through over medium heat, about 5 minutes.

Stir in cream just before serving. Ladle into serving bowls and top with crisp parsnip chips.

Serves 6

Spicy squash and bean soup

2 tablespoons olive oil

3 scallions (shallots/spring onions), finely sliced

12 oz (375 g) carrots, peeled and sliced

5 oz (150 g) rutabaga (swede), peeled and cubed

2 sticks celery, sliced

1 lb (500 g) butternut squash (pumpkin), peeled and cubed

1 small red chili pepper, seeded and sliced

5 oz (150 g) drained, canned cannellini beans

6 cups (48 fl oz/1.5 L) vegetable stock (see page 11)

1 bay leaf

1 cup (8 fl oz/250 ml) light (single) cream

4 tablespoons chopped fresh mint, for garnish

2 tablespoons chopped cilantro (fresh coriander) leaves, for garnish

Warm olive oil in a large saucepan over medium heat. Add scallions, carrots, rutabaga, celery, squash and chili pepper and cook until vegetables soften slightly, about 6 minutes. Add beans, stock, bay leaf and cilantro. Bring to a boil. Cover, reduce heat to low and cook until vegetables are tender, about 15 minutes.

Working in batches, puree soup in a food processor. Return soup to the pan and heat through, about 3 minutes. Ladle into bowls and swirl 1/4 cup (2 fl oz/60 ml) cream into each serving. Garnish with herbs and serve immediately.

Serves 4

Creamy beet and potato borscht

2 oz (60g) butter

2 large yellow (brown) onions, peeled and chopped

1 large carrot, peeled and chopped

1 lb (500 g) cooked beets (beetroot), diced

12 oz (375 g) potatoes, peeled and diced

grated zest of 1/2 lemon

2 tablespoons lemon juice

5 cups (40 fl oz/1.25 L) beef or vegetable stock (see page 11)

salt and freshly ground black pepper, to taste

1/2 level teaspoon ground fenugreek

1 1/4 cups (10 fl oz/300 ml) milk

1–2 level tablespoons finely chopped chives or scallion (shallot/spring onion) tops

2/3 cup (5 oz/165 ml) sour cream

Melt butter in a saucepan and sauté onion and carrot very gently, stirring frequently, until beginning to soften but not brown, 7–8 minutes. Add beets, potato, lemon zest and juice, stock, seasonings and fenugreek and bring to a boil. Cover and simmer until very tender, about 30 minutes. Cool slightly.

Sieve the soup or puree in a food processor. Transfer to a clean pan. Add milk and bring back to a boil. Adjust seasonings and stir in chives or scallion tops.

Serve each bowl of soup with a spoonful of sour cream swirled through.

Serves 6

Potato and watercress soup

2 oz (60 g) butter
8 scallions (shallots/spring onions), trimmed and sliced
12 oz (375 g) potatoes, peeled and diced
2 bunches watercress, trimmed and roughly chopped
3 cups (24 fl oz/750 ml) chicken or vegetable stock
   (see pages 10 and 11)
salt and freshly ground black pepper, to taste
½ teaspoon Worcestershire sauce
2 teaspoons lemon juice
1¼ cups (10 fl oz/300 ml) milk
6 tablespoons light (single) cream
6 tablespoons plain (natural) yogurt
watercress sprigs, for garnish

Melt butter in a large saucepan and sauté scallions and potato gently for a few minutes without browning. Add watercress to pan and toss. Add stock, seasonings, Worcestershire sauce and lemon juice and bring to a boil. Reduce heat, cover, and simmer gently until tender, about 30 minutes. Cool slightly and either sieve the soup or puree in a food processor.

   Return soup to a clean pan. Stir in milk and bring soup back to a boil for about 1 minute. Thoroughly blend cream and yogurt, and add about half to the soup. Reheat gently and adjust seasonings. Serve each portion with a spoonful of remaining cream and yogurt mixture swirled through it, and topped with watercress.
Serves 6

Creamed squash and potato soup

2 oz (60 g) butter
2 yellow (brown) onions, sliced
1 clove garlic, crushed
2 lb (1 kg) butternut squash (pumpkin), peeled, seeded
   and diced
12 oz (375 g) potatoes, peeled and diced
1½ teaspoons tomato paste
2½ cups (20 fl oz/625 ml) chicken or vegetable stock
   (see pages 10 and 11)
salt and freshly ground black pepper, to taste
2 teaspoons lemon or lime juice
½ teaspoon ground allspice
2½ cups (20 fl oz/625 ml) milk
6 tablespoons sour cream
chopped fresh parsley leaves, for garnish (optional)

Melt butter in a large saucepan and sauté onion and garlic very gently until soft but not browned. Add squash and potatoes and cook for a few minutes, then add tomato paste, stock, seasonings, lemon or lime juice and allspice and bring to a boil. Cover pan and simmer gently until very tender, about 40 minutes.

   Sieve soup or puree in a food processor, and transfer to a clean pan. Add milk and bring back to a boil, whisking continuously. Reduce heat and simmer for 2–3 minutes. Adjust seasonings and stir in sour cream, then reheat. Serve sprinkled with parsley.
Serves 6

Cream of tomato soup

8–10 plum (Roma) tomatoes, peeled, or 2 x 14 oz
   (440 g) cans tomatoes, with juice

2 teaspoons sugar

1 teaspoon salt

2 tablespoons all-purpose (plain) flour

1 tablespoon vegetable oil

2 teaspoons ground coriander

2 teaspoons cumin

½ teaspoon cayenne pepper or chili powder, or to taste

1 cup (8 fl oz/250 ml) heavy (double) cream

freshly ground black pepper, to taste

chopped cilantro (fresh coriander) or basil leaves,
   for garnish

chopped fresh tomato, for garnish (optional)

Puree tomatoes, sugar, salt and flour in a food processor.

Heat oil in a saucepan. Add spices and cook until fragrant, about 1 minute. Add cream and pureed tomatoes. Simmer, stirring, for a few minutes, until slightly thickened. Season with pepper.

Serve sprinkled with cilantro or basil and fresh tomato for garnish, if desired.

Serves 2–4

Variation

For Tomato and coconut soup, replace the cream with 1 cup (8 fl oz/250 ml) coconut cream.

Curried split pea soup

1 cup (6½ oz/200 g) dried split peas
3 cups (24 fl oz/750 ml) cold water
1 tablespoon olive oil
2 onions, chopped
2 cloves garlic, crushed
2 teaspoons curry powder
1 carrot, peeled and diced
1 boiling potato, peeled and diced
4 cups (32 fl oz/1 L) vegetable stock (see page 11)
½ teaspoon salt
½ teaspoon ground black pepper
1 cup (8 oz/250 g) plain (natural) yogurt
fresh mint leaves, for garnish

Pick over peas and remove any that are discolored. Rinse in a colander under cold running water. Put peas in a medium saucepan with cold water. Bring to a boil, reduce heat and simmer until tender, about 30 minutes. Drain peas in a colander.

In a large saucepan over medium heat, heat oil and sauté onions until golden brown, about 3 minutes.

Add garlic and cook for 1 minute, then add curry powder, stirring for 30 seconds. Add carrot, potato, peas, stock, salt and pepper. Simmer until vegetables are cooked, about 30 minutes. Just before serving, taste and adjust seasoning.

Stir yogurt through hot soup and ladle into soup bowls. Garnish with mint leaves.

Serves 6–8

Creamy squash and leek soup

2 teaspoons vegetable oil
2 yellow (brown) onions, chopped
2 cloves garlic, crushed
2 leeks, washed and thinly sliced
1 lb (500 g) butternut squash (pumpkin), peeled and diced
1 boiling potato, peeled and diced
1 tablespoon tomato paste
4 cups (32 fl oz/1 L) vegetable stock (see page 11)
½ teaspoon ground white pepper
1 tablespoon fresh lemon juice
¼ cup (2 oz/60 g) plain (natural) low-fat yogurt
1 tablespoon chopped fresh flat-leaf (Italian) parsley, for garnish

In a large, heavy-based saucepan over low heat, heat oil and cook onions and garlic until tender, about 5 minutes. Add leeks and cook for 5 minutes. Add squash, potato, tomato paste and vegetable stock. Cover and bring to a boil, then reduce heat and simmer for 25 minutes.

Transfer mixture to a food processor and process until smooth, stopping and scraping down sides of container as needed. Stir in pepper and lemon juice. Ladle warm soup into bowls. Spoon 2 teaspoons yogurt into center of each portion and garnish with parsley.

Serves 6

LEFT Creamy squash and leek soup

Steamed squash soup with hazelnuts

4 golden nugget butternut squash (pumpkin),
   3½ lb (1.8 kg) in total
1 tablespoon butter or vegetable oil
2 cloves garlic, crushed
1 small yellow (brown) onion, chopped
1 teaspoon peeled and grated fresh ginger
4 cups (32 fl oz/1 L) chicken or vegetable stock
   (see pages 10 and 11)
salt and freshly ground black pepper, to taste
4 teaspoons plain (natural) yogurt or sour cream,
   for garnish
12 sprigs watercress, for garnish
½ cup (2½ oz/75 g) hazelnuts, toasted, skinned and
   coarsely chopped, for garnish

Partially fill a large wok or pot with water and bring to a rapid simmer. Place whole squash in oiled steamer. Place steamer over water, cover, and steam until squash are just tender, 40–45 minutes. Remove steamer from wok before removing squash.

Place squash on a board, flatter side down (take care, as they will be hot). Cut tops off and discard. Discard seeds, and scoop out flesh to within ¼ in (6 mm) of skin, being careful not to break through. Turn squash upside down to drain, adding any drained juice to flesh. Place flesh in a food processor, in batches, and puree. Cover shells with foil to keep warm.

Heat butter or vegetable oil in a medium saucepan over medium heat. Cook garlic, onion and ginger until softened but not brown, 4–5 minutes. Add pureed squash, stock, and salt and pepper, and simmer for 10 minutes.

Pour soup into shells and serve garnished with yogurt, watercress and hazelnuts.
Serves 4

Hint
Squash and soup can be prepared the day before serving and chilled. If reheating soup in a saucepan, steam squash for 10–15 minutes to heat through before filling with hot soup.

Cream of spinach soup

3 packs (about 1½ lb/750 g) frozen spinach, chopped

2 tablespoons butter or olive oil

1 small yellow (brown) onion, finely chopped

1 clove garlic, finely chopped

2 tablespoons all-purpose (plain) flour

4 cups (32 fl oz/1 L) chicken stock (see page 10)

salt and freshly ground black pepper, to taste

½ teaspoon ground nutmeg, or to taste

1 cup (8 fl oz/250 ml) light (single) cream

cayenne pepper or hot pepper sauce, to taste,
    for serving

Place frozen spinach in a saucepan, cover, and cook gently for 10 minutes or until softened. Drain well and transfer to a food processor.

Place butter, onion and garlic in a saucepan and cook until onion is soft. Sprinkle in flour, and stir until onion is golden. Add stock and boil for 5 minutes, stirring.

Add half this liquid to spinach in food processor and puree until smooth. Return spinach mixture to pan and season with salt, pepper and nutmeg. Add cream and heat gently – do not boil.

Serve with a sprinkle of cayenne or a dash of hot pepper sauce.

Serves 4

Variations

Scatter smoked salmon, chopped or cut into thin strips, on top.

If you prefer something more flavorsome, try adding spices with the onion: 1 teaspoon ground cumin, 2 teaspoons mustard seeds, 2 teaspoons chopped ginger, 1 chopped garlic clove, 1 chopped red chili pepper.

Experiment with the taste of ground fenugreek, ground cloves and ground cinnamon – start with ¼ teaspoon of any of these.

Pea and lettuce soup

2 lb (1 kg) peas in their pods
2 tablespoons vegetable oil
2 medium leeks, trimmed, washed and cut into
   ½ in (12 mm) pieces
2 large potatoes, peeled and cut into ½ in (12 mm)
   cubes
½ teaspoon sugar
4 cups (32 fl oz/1 L) vegetable stock (see page 11)
1 head iceberg lettuce, trimmed and chopped
⅓ cup (3 fl oz/90 ml) crème fraîche
1 tablespoon chopped chives, for garnish (optional)

Remove peas from pods and discard pods. Warm oil in
a large saucepan over medium heat. Add leek and
potato and cook for 2 minutes, stirring constantly. Add
peas, sugar and stock. Increase heat to bring mixture
to a boil, then reduce heat to medium–low—liquid
should be at a steady simmer. Cover and simmer for
10 minutes.

   Stir in lettuce, and cover. Cook until potatoes are
tender, about 3 minutes.

   Pour soup into a large bowl. Working in batches, ladle
soup into food processor and process until smooth,
about 30 seconds. Return soup to pan and stir over low
heat until heated through, about 3 minutes.

   Serve in heated bowls, topping each serving with
crème fraîche and chives, if using.

Serves 4–6

Caldo verde
(Spinach soup)

2 tablespoons vegetable oil

2 yellow (brown) onions, thinly sliced

4 cloves garlic, crushed

½ teaspoon ground turmeric

1 bunch spinach, trimmed, rinsed well and chopped

1½ cups (12 fl oz/375 ml) milk

1½ cups (12 fl oz/375 ml) chicken or vegetable stock
   (see pages 10 and 11) or water

1 tablespoon butter

½ teaspoon freshly grated nutmeg

salt and freshly ground black pepper, to taste

heavy (double) cream, for garnish

In a large, heavy-based saucepan, heat oil over medium heat. Add onions and cook, stirring occasionally, until softened, about 5 minutes. Add garlic and turmeric and cook, stirring, for 30 seconds. Add spinach to pan and cook, tossing, just until spinach wilts. Remove from heat and let cool.

Place spinach mixture in a food processor and process to a smooth puree, adding a small amount of milk if necessary. Return mixture to pan. Stir in remaining milk and stock or water, and bring to a simmer over medium heat. Simmer, uncovered, for 3 minutes. Add butter and nutmeg and season with salt and pepper. Simmer for 2 minutes.

Ladle into bowls and add a swirl of cream to each bowl.

Serves 4–6

Cream of
broccoli soup

2 tablespoons butter

8 oz (250 g) yellow (brown) onions, chopped

4 oz (125 g) carrot, peeled and sliced

4 oz (125 g) celery, sliced

1–2 heads broccoli, trimmed and roughly chopped

4 cups (32 fl oz/1 L) chicken or vegetable stock
   (see pages 10 and 11)

¾ cup (6 fl oz/180 ml) milk

¼ cup (2 fl oz/60 ml) light (single) cream

2 teaspoons lemon juice

salt and freshly ground black pepper, to taste

Melt butter in a large saucepan over low heat. Add onion, carrot and celery and cook, stirring, about 5 minutes. Add broccoli and stock and bring to a boil. Cover and simmer until vegetables are tender, about 30 minutes.

Transfer to a food processor and puree until smooth. Return to pan over medium heat and stir in milk, cream, lemon juice and seasoning. Cook, stirring, until thickened.

Serves 6

LEFT Caldo verde (Spinach soup)

Du Barry soup

2 oz (60 g) butter

1 large yellow (brown) onion, peeled and chopped
    finely

1 small cauliflower, 1½–2 lb (750 g–1 kg), trimmed and
    cut into rough florets

12 oz (375 g) potatoes, peeled and diced

2½ cups (20 fl oz/625 ml) chicken or vegetable stock
    (see pages 10 and 11)

salt and freshly ground black pepper, to taste

a little freshly grated nutmeg

1 bay leaf

2 cups (16 fl oz/500 ml) milk

1 tablespoon lemon juice, or to taste

⅓ cup (3 fl oz/90 ml) light (single) cream

2 tablespoons chopped fresh chervil

fresh chervil leaves, for garnish

toasted flaked almonds, for garnish

Melt butter in a large saucepan and sauté onion very
gently until soft but not browned, about 5 minutes. Add
cauliflower and potato to pan and cook gently for
2–3 minutes. Add stock, seasonings, nutmeg and bay
leaf and bring to a boil. Cover and simmer until tender,
about 30 minutes. Discard bay leaf.

Sieve the soup or puree in a food processor. Return
to a clean pan, then add milk and lemon juice and
simmer for 3–4 minutes. Stir in cream and chopped
chervil and reheat gently. Adjust seasonings and serve
sprinkled with fresh chervil leaves and toasted almonds.

Serves 6

Potato and cauliflower soup

2 oz (60 g) butter

2 yellow (brown) onions, chopped

1 leek, sliced

1 large potato, peeled and chopped

1 cauliflower, cut into florets

5 cups (40 fl oz/1¼ L) chicken or vegetable stock
    (see pages 10 and 11)

½-1 cup (2-4 oz/60-125 g) grated cheese

salt and freshly ground black pepper, to taste

fried bacon chips or chopped fresh chives, for garnish

fried croutons, for garnish (see page 67)

Melt butter in a large saucepan and cook onion and
leek, stirring, until soft, about 5 minutes. Add potato,
cauliflower and stock and bring to a boil. Cover and
simmer until vegetables are tender, about 30 minutes.

Transfer to a food processor and puree until smooth.
Return to pan over medium heat and add cheese. Stir
through until melted.

Serve in individual bowls garnished with bacon chips
or chives and croutons.

Serves 6

RIGHT Potato and cauliflower soup

Chicken and duck

Chicken laksa

2 large skinless, boneless chicken breast halves,
   1 lb (500 g) in total
2 tablespoons light olive oil
sea salt and freshly ground black pepper, to taste
½ cup (4 oz/125 g) laksa paste (see page 13)
3 tablespoons lemon or lime juice
3 cups (24 fl oz/750 ml) coconut milk
3 cups (24 fl oz/750 ml) chicken stock (see page 10)
10 oz (300 g) cherry tomatoes
6 oz (180 g) thick dried rice noodles
1 cup (5 oz (150 g) pineapple pieces, about
   ½ in (12 mm)
1 small cucumber, peeled and sliced
2 tablespoons chopped fresh mint leaves
¼ cup (⅓ oz/10 g) cilantro (fresh coriander) leaves
¼ cup crispy fried shallots (French shallots), for garnish
   (see page 92)

Brush chicken breasts with 2 teaspoons of olive oil. Heat a cast-iron frying pan or stove-top grill pan over high heat until very hot, about 5 minutes. Cook chicken breasts until tender and cooked through, 4–5 minutes on each side. Season with salt and black pepper. Remove and set aside.

Heat remaining oil in a large saucepan over medium–high heat. Stir in laksa paste and cook stirring frequently until fragrant, 4–5 minutes. Add lime or lemon juice, coconut milk and chicken stock and stir until mixture is thoroughly combined. Reduce heat to medium and simmer for 10 minutes. Add tomatoes and simmer for 5 minutes.

Place noodles in a large bowl and add enough boiling water to cover. Allow to stand until noodles are soft, about 3 minutes. Drain noodles, rinse under warm water and set aside.

Slice chicken breasts into thin slices. Spoon noodles into individual bowls and ladle soup over them. Top with chicken slices and remaining ingredients, finishing with a sprinkling of shallots. Serve immediately.

Serves 4

Chicken and mushroom soup

4 dried Chinese mushrooms

4 cups (32 fl oz/1 L) chicken stock (see page 10)

2 cloves garlic, crushed

1 teaspoon peeled and grated ginger

1 tablespoon rice vinegar

2 teaspoons palm sugar or brown sugar

1 chicken fillet, about 5 oz (150 g), thinly sliced

6 scallions (shallots/spring onions), chopped

2 stalks lemongrass, bruised and sliced

1 small red chili pepper, seeded and chopped

Place mushrooms in small bowl, add enough boiling water to cover. Allow to stand until softened, 10–15 minutes. Drain, then squeeze excess liquid from mushrooms. Slice mushrooms thinly, discarding thick stems.

Place chicken stock, garlic, ginger, vinegar and sugar in wok. Bring to a boil, reduce heat to low and simmer, uncovered, for 5 minutes. Stir in sliced mushrooms, chicken, scallions, lemongrass and chili pepper. Simmer until chicken is opaque, about 15 minutes.

Serve hot, ladled into bowls.

Serves 4

Sweet potato chowder with chicken

2 oz (60 g) butter

1 large yellow (brown) onion, peeled and finely chopped

2 sticks celery, finely chopped

¼ cup (1 oz/30 g) all-purpose (plain) flour, sifted

2 teaspoons tomato paste

½–1 teaspoon medium curry powder (optional)

5 cups (40 fl oz/1.25 L) chicken stock (see page 10)

2–3 carrots, peeled and finely chopped or
    coarsely grated

1 x 12 oz (375 g) can corn kernels, drained

1 small red bell pepper (capsicum), seeded
    and chopped

12 oz (375 g) sweet potatoes, peeled and
    finely chopped

3 oz (90 g) cooked chicken, finely chopped

1 teaspoon Worcestershire sauce

4 tablespoons chopped fresh flat-leaf (Italian) parsley

Melt butter in a large saucepan and sauté onion and celery gently until soft but not browned, about 5 minutes. Stir in flour, tomato paste and curry powder (if using) and cook for 1–2 minutes, then gradually add chicken stock and bring to a boil.

Add carrot, corn, bell pepper, sweet potato and chicken, together with seasonings and Worcestershire sauce, and simmer gently until tender and fairly thick, about 20 minutes. Adjust seasoning and stir 2 tablespoons of parsley into the chowder.

Serve very hot, sprinkled with remaining parsley and accompanied by hot crusty bread or rolls.

Serves 4–6

Variation

For a vegetarian soup, omit chopped chicken and use vegetable stock.

Chicken and coconut milk soup

2 cups (16 fl oz/500 ml) coconut cream

1 cup (8 fl oz/250 ml) coconut milk

2 stalks lemongrass, white part only, outer leaves
   discarded and cut into 1 in (2.5 cm) pieces

1 x ½ in (12 mm) piece galangal, thinly sliced

2 tablespoons coarsely chopped shallots
   (French shallots), preferably pink

10–15 small fresh chili peppers, halved lengthwise

4 oz (125 g) canned or 8 oz (250 g) fresh straw
   mushrooms, rinsed, drained and halved

12 oz (375 g) boneless, skinless chicken breasts,
   thinly sliced

2–3 tablespoons fish sauce, to taste

3 fresh kaffir lime leaves, stemmed

½ cup (¾ oz/20 g) coarsely chopped cilantro
   (fresh coriander)

2 tablespoons fresh lime juice

2 scallions (shallots/spring onions), chopped,
   for garnish

In a wok or large saucepan over high heat, combine coconut cream, coconut milk, lemongrass, galangal, shallots, chilies and mushrooms. Bring to a boil, reduce heat, and simmer for 3–5 minutes. Add chicken, stirring well. Add fish sauce and lime leaves. Return to a boil. Add half the cilantro and turn off heat. Stir in lime juice.

Transfer to bowls for serving, garnish with scallions and remaining cilantro. Serve.

Serves 4–6

Hints

For a less rich soup, replace the coconut cream with an equal quantity of coconut milk. For a less spicy broth, keep the chili peppers whole.

Note

Chicken and coconut milk soup (Tom kha gai) is one of Thailand's best-known soups, with a creamy consistency and a lovely lemony flavor. The fibrous ingredients in this dish – kaffir lime leaf, galangal and lemongrass – are not eaten. Just push them aside.

Chicken vermicelli soup with egg

8 oz (250 g) carrots, peeled and cut into tiny cubes

8 oz (250 g) leeks, thinly sliced

5 cups (40 fl oz/1.25 L) chicken stock

4 oz (125 g) cooked chicken, shredded

2 oz (60 g) vermicelli

2 eggs

juice of ½ lemon

freshly ground black pepper, to taste

Put carrots and leeks into a large saucepan with stock. Bring to a boil, reduce heat, cover, and simmer for 10 minutes.

Add chicken and vermicelli and cook for a further 5 minutes.

In a bowl, mix eggs and lemon juice. Add ½ cup (4 fl oz/125 ml) stock from the pan, mix well, then strain back into the pan.

Reheat soup gently, stirring constantly, but do not allow to boil. Adjust seasoning.

Serves 4

Chicken and sweet corn soup

2 teaspoons light olive or vegetable oil

1 large yellow (brown) onion, sliced

1 lb (500 g) skinless, boneless chicken thigh meat, cut
into 1 in (2.5 cm) cubes

4 oz (125 g) sliced ham, cut into thick strips

2 cloves garlic, chopped

1 x 2 in (5 cm) piece fresh ginger, peeled and grated

1½ lb (750 g) fresh or frozen corn kernels

8 cups (64 fl oz/2 L) chicken stock (see page 10)

½ teaspoon white pepper, or to taste

sea salt, to taste

1 small red (Spanish) onion, cut into petals (see Hints),
for garnish

4 small red chili peppers, cut to form flowers
(see Hints), for garnish

8 baby sweet corn cobs, fresh or canned, for garnish

Heat oil in a large saucepan over medium–high heat.
Add onion and cook until soft and slightly golden, about
5 minutes, stirring occasionally.

Add chicken cubes, ham strips, garlic and ginger and
continue to cook for 2–3 minutes. Add corn kernels and
cook for a further 2 minutes. Add chicken stock and
bring mixture to a boil.

Reduce heat to medium and simmer until corn is soft,
about 10 minutes. Season to taste with white pepper
and salt.

Ladle into individual bowls and garnish with red onion
petals, chili pepper flowers and baby corn cobs.

Serves 4

Hints

To make onion petals, halve onion, cutting from root end
to top, then cut each half, from just above root end to
top, into thick wedges. The root end should hold
wedges together. Separate layers, without breaking from
root end, so you have individual petals.

To make chili flowers, cut chili peppers into strips,
from tip to just next to stem, and place in a bowl of ice
water in the refrigerator until strips curl, 20–30 minutes.

Vietnamese chicken and rice soup

8 cups (64 fl oz/2 L) chicken or pho beef stock
  (see pages 10 and 11)
12 oz (375 g) boneless, skinless chicken thighs or
  breasts, thinly sliced
1 cup (6½ oz/200 g) uncooked rice, preferably
  jasmine rice
¼ cup (2 fl oz/60 ml) vegetable oil
1 teaspoon ground black pepper
¼ bunch (⅔ oz/20 g) Chinese (flat/garlic) chives,
  coarsely chopped
½ cup (2 oz/60 g) crispy fried shallots (French shallots)
  (see page 92)
fish sauce, to taste

In a large pot over high heat, bring stock to a boil. Add chicken and cook, 2–3 minutes for thigh meat or 1–2 minutes for breast meat. Using a skimmer, transfer chicken to a bowl.

Meanwhile, rinse rice in several changes of cold water until water is no longer cloudy. Drain and gradually stir into boiling stock. Reduce heat to low and cook, uncovered and stirring occasionally, until just tender, about 15 minutes.

At the last minute, add cooked chicken pieces to stock. Stir to combine, then ladle into warmed soup bowls. Sprinkle with black pepper and garnish with chives and fried shallots. Serve with fish sauce for each diner to add to taste.

Serves 6

Variation: With fish

Replace stock with Fish stock (see page 12) and substitute an equal quantity of fish fillets, cut into 1 in (2.5 cm) pieces, for chicken pieces. Garnish with chives, plus ¼ cup (⅓ oz/10 g) coarsely chopped dill and serve with fish sauce for each diner to add to taste.

Chicken soup

1 x 5 lb (2.5 kg) chicken, cut into pieces
2 yellow (brown) onions, halved
3 carrots, peeled and cut into thick slices
1 stick celery, including green leaves, halved
1 parsnip, peeled and chopped
8 sprigs fresh flat-leaf (Italian) parsley
3 sprigs fresh dill
1 tablespoon coarse salt
10 black peppercorns
dumplings or egg noodles, for serving (optional)

Wash chicken thoroughly and cut off excess fat. Place chicken in a large saucepan and add enough water to cover. Bring to a boil and cook, skimming off foam and scum as necessary, for 15 minutes. Add onions, carrots, celery, parsnip, parsley, dill, salt and peppercorns. Return to a boil, then reduce heat and simmer for 2½–3 hours. Let cool and strain through a sieve. Refrigerate soup overnight.

Next day, remove and discard fat from top of soup. Heat soup and adjust seasoning. Serve with dumplings or egg noodles, if desired.

Serves 6–8

Hot and sour chicken soup

2 teaspoons peanut oil

1 red onion, sliced

1 medium carrot, peeled and julienned

2–4 skinless, boneless chicken breasts,
8 oz (250 g) each, sliced

3 oz (90 g) small button mushrooms, sliced (optional)

8 cups (64 fl oz/2 L) hot and sour soup stock
(see page 13)

4 fresh or 8 dried kaffir lime leaves

lime juice and fish sauce, to taste

4 sprigs basil, for garnish

Heat peanut oil in a large saucepan over medium heat
until hot, about 1 minute. Add onion and carrot. Cook,
stirring, until just soft, 4–5 minutes. Add chicken,
mushrooms if using and stock and bring to a steady
simmer. Add lime leaves and simmer until chicken is
cooked through, about 10 minutes. Season to taste with
lime juice and fish sauce, 1 teaspoon at a time. Remove
lime leaves.

Ladle into individual bowls and serve each bowl
garnished with a sprig of basil.

Serves 4

Chicken and noodle soup

4 dried Chinese mushrooms

8 oz (250 g) egg noodles

2 oz (60 g) snow peas (mange-tout), shredded

1 tablespoon vegetable oil

1 tablespoon light soy sauce

1 tablespoon rice wine

4 cups (32 fl oz/1 L) chicken stock (see page 10)

8 oz (250 g) cooked skinless chicken meat, shredded

2 oz (60 g) fresh bean sprouts, rinsed, for garnish

Place mushrooms in a small bowl and add enough boiling water to cover. Allow to stand until softened, 10–15 minutes. Drain mushrooms, then squeeze out excess liquid. Thinly slice mushrooms, discarding tough stems.

Cook egg noodles as directed on package. Drain and set aside.

Place mange-tout in a bowl and add enough boiling water to cover. Let stand for 1 minute, then drain. Refresh mange-tout immediately in cold water.

In a wok or saucepan over medium–high heat, warm oil. Add sliced mushrooms and stir-fry for 1 minute. Add noodles, snow peas, soy sauce, rice wine, stock and shredded chicken. Bring to a boil over medium–high heat, stirring occasionally.

Ladle into individual bowls, and garnish each serving with bean sprouts.

Serves 4

Ramen noodle and roast duck soup

6½ oz (200 g) ramen noodles

2 cups (16 fl oz/500 ml) chicken stock (see page 10)

3 cups (24 fl oz/750 ml) water

5 thin slices peeled fresh ginger

4 small red chili peppers, halved and seeded (if desired)

2 teaspoons lime juice

3 stalks lemongrass, bruised

3 cilantro (fresh coriander) roots, bruised

1 Chinese roast duck, meat removed and chopped

4 scallions (shallots/spring onions), chopped

2 oz (60 g) fresh bean sprouts, rinsed, for garnish

¼ cup (⅓ oz/10 g) chopped cilantro (fresh coriander),
for garnish

Cook noodles as directed on package. Drain and set aside. Place stock, water, ginger, 4 chili pepper halves and lime juice in a saucepan. Bring to a boil, reduce heat to low, cover and simmer, stirring occasionally, until flavors are blended, about 5 minutes. Add lemongrass and cilantro roots. Simmer, stirring occasionally, for 15 minutes. Strain through a fine-meshed sieve. Return stock to pan.

Add duck meat, scallions and noodles to stock and simmer until heated through, about 5 minutes.

Ladle into individual bowls. Top each serving with bean sprouts, chopped cilantro and remaining chili pepper halves.

Serves 4

Hint

Chinese roast duck is readily available at Asian markets. Be sure to ask for the duck whole, not chopped on the bone.

Roast duck and sweet potato soup

2 medium sweet potatoes

1½ tablespoons light olive oil

2 large red onions, very thinly sliced

3 cloves garlic, crushed

1 x 2 in (5 cm) piece fresh ginger, peeled and grated

8 cups (64 fl oz/2 L) chicken stock (see page 10)

2 small red chili peppers, thinly sliced

grated zest of 1 lime

1 Chinese roast duck, meat removed from bones

1 teaspoon fish sauce

2 tablespoons lime juice

freshly ground black pepper, to taste

½ cup (½ oz/15 g) cilantro (fresh coriander) leaves plus
    4 sprigs

½ cup (½ oz/15 g) small basil leaves

½ cup (½ oz/15 g) small mint leaves

Preheat oven to 400°F (200°C/Gas 6). Place sweet potatoes on an oven rack and bake until a skewer inserted through thickest part meets with no resistance, 30–40 minutes. Remove sweet potatoes from oven and set aside to cool. When cool enough to handle, remove skin and chop flesh into pieces.

Heat 1 tablespoon of oil in a large saucepan over medium heat. Add half the onion slices, half the garlic and half the ginger and cook, stirring, for 3–4 minutes. Add chicken stock and bring liquid to a steady simmer. Simmer for 15 minutes. Reduce heat to medium–low, add chopped sweet potato and cook for 2–3 minutes. Remove from heat and allow to cool slightly. Place mixture, working in batches, in a food processor and puree until smooth, about 3 minutes. Return pureed mixture to a large saucepan and keep warm until ready to serve.

Heat remaining oil in a large frying pan or wok. Add remaining onion, garlic and ginger, chili peppers, lime zest and duck and cook, tossing and stirring, for 1 minute. Remove from heat and add fish sauce, lime juice, black pepper, cilantro, basil and mint. Stir until combined.

Ladle soup into individual bowls, top with duck mixture and serve immediately.

Serves 4

Beef and pork

Classic beef pho

12 oz (375 g) lean beef fillet

10 oz (300 g) fresh thick rice noodles

6 oz (180 g) small green beans, trimmed

6 oz (180 g) snow peas (mange-tout), trimmed

1 small bunch cilantro (fresh coriander), separated into sprigs

1 cup (1 oz/30 g) small basil leaves

5 oz (150 g) bean sprouts, trimmed

8 cups (64 fl oz/2 L) beef pho stock (see page 11)

1 lime, quartered

chili paste or sambal oelek, to taste

2 tablespoons fish sauce, to taste (optional)

Wrap beef fillet in plastic wrap and freeze until partially frozen, about 1 hour. Remove from freezer and slice as thinly as possible. Set aside at room temperature and allow to defrost completely.

Bring a large pot of water to a boil and add rice noodles. Cook until noodles are tender, 3–4 minutes. Drain noodles in a colander and set aside.

Bring a small saucepan with 1 in (2.5 cm) water to a boil. Add green beans and snow peas and cook for 1 minute. Drain immediately and place in a bowl with cilantro, basil and bean sprouts. Set aside.

Heat stock in a large saucepan until boiling. Rinse noodles under very hot water quickly, using a fork to separate them. Divide among 4 bowls. Pour stock over noodles and top with beef slices.

Allow to stand for 1–2 minutes. Top with herbs and vegetables. Add a squeeze of lime, and chili paste or sambal oelek and fish sauce (if using).

Serves 4

Quick beef and pepper soup

2 tablespoons olive oil

1 yellow (brown) onion, chopped

12 oz (375 g) lean braising steak (chuck or blade),
    cut into very small dice

1 tablespoon paprika

1 fennel, about 8 oz (250 g), cut into small dice

salt and freshly ground black pepper, to taste

4 cups (32 fl oz/1 L) beef stock (see page 11)

1 large red bell pepper (capsicum), seeded and cut
    into diamond shapes

1 large yellow bell pepper (capsicum), seeded and cut
    into diamond shapes

2 tablespoons chopped fresh parsley, for garnish

Heat oil in a large saucepan and sauté onion until soft,
about 2 minutes. Add beef and cook until browned. Stir
in paprika, fennel, seasonings and stock and bring to a
boil. Cover pan, reduce heat and simmer for 20 minutes.

Add bell peppers and cook for a further 10 minutes.

Divide soup among 4 warmed soup bowls, sprinkle
with chopped parsley and serve.

Serves 4

Meatball soup

1 lb (500 g) finely ground (minced) beef
1 small yellow (brown) onion, finely chopped
1 egg, beaten
⅓ cup (2½ oz/75 g) medium-grain rice
2 tablespoons finely chopped fresh flat-leaf (Italian)
    parsley
salt and freshly ground black pepper, to taste
all-purpose (plain) flour, for coating
5 cups (40 fl oz/1.25 L) beef or chicken stock
    (see pages 10 and 11)

1 tablespoon butter
2 eggs
juice of 1 lemon
chopped fresh flat-leaf (Italian) parsley, for garnish
crusty bread, for serving

In a bowl, mix beef, onion, egg, rice, finely chopped parsley and salt and pepper. Shape into meatballs the size of a small walnut and coat lightly with flour.

Bring stock to a boil in a pot, season with salt and pepper (if necessary) and drop in meatballs. Add butter. Cover and simmer for 1 hour.

In a bowl, beat eggs until light and foamy. Gradually beat in lemon juice. Slowly add 2 cups (16 fl oz/500 ml) simmering stock, beating constantly.

Pour egg mixture into soup and stir constantly over low heat to cook egg, for 2 minutes. Remove soup from heat and stir for 1 minute longer so the heat of the pot will not cause the egg to curdle.

Ladle soup into deep soup bowls and sprinkle with chopped parsley. Serve with bread.

Serves 6

Borscht

1–2 tablespoons oil
1 red onion, chopped
1 lb (500 g) lean stewing steak (chuck steak),
   cut into small cubes
1 lb (500 g) raw beets (beetroot), peeled and grated
12 oz (375 g) red cabbage, finely shredded
5 cups (40 fl oz/1.25 L) beef stock (see page 11)
2 tablespoons red wine vinegar
1 tablespoon ketchup (tomato sauce)
salt and freshly ground black pepper, to taste
1 teaspoon dried thyme
8 oz (250 g) firm waxy potatoes, peeled and diced
½ cup (4 fl oz/125 ml) low-fat sour cream
1 teaspoon fennel seeds, for garnish
2 teaspoons chopped fresh dill, for garnish

In a large saucepan, heat oil, then add onion and beef,
cover, and cook until beef is brown.

   Add beets, cabbage, beef stock, vinegar, ketchup,
seasonings and thyme. Bring to a boil, then reduce heat
and simmer for 40 minutes.

   Add potatoes to pan and cook for a further
10 minutes.

   Divide the soup among warmed bowls. Put
1 tablespoon sour cream into the middle of each, then
sprinkle with fennel seeds and dill.

Serves 4–6

Beef and barley soup

2 tablespoons vegetable oil
4 cloves garlic, crushed
1 large yellow (brown) onion, diced
1 leek, thinly sliced, including some light green section
1 lb (500 g) lean stewing steak (chuck steak), cut into
   ½ in (12 mm) cubes
¾ cup (4½ oz/135 g) pearl barley, rinsed
4 large carrots, 1 lb (500 g) in total, peeled and diced
2 vine-ripened tomatoes, diced
10 cups (80 fl oz/2.5 L) beef stock (see page 11)
2 large boiling potatoes, peeled and diced
1 teaspoon salt
½ teaspoon ground pepper
2 tablespoons chopped fresh flat-leaf (Italian) parsley,
   for garnish

In a large saucepan or soup pot, heat oil and sauté
garlic, onion and leek until translucent but not brown,
about 10 minutes.

   Add meat, barley, carrots, tomatoes and stock. Bring
to a boil, then simmer for 1½ hours.

   Add potatoes, salt and pepper and cook until meat is
fork tender and barley is soft, about 30 minutes. Taste
and adjust seasoning.

   Serve hot, garnished with parsley.

Serves 8

LEFT Borscht

Beef and cabbage soup

1 red chili pepper

4 shallots (French shallots), peeled

2 cloves garlic

1 teaspoon galangal powder or 1 tablespoon chopped
   fresh galangal or fresh ginger

½ cup (½ oz/15 g) cilantro (fresh coriander) leaves

2 tablespoons finely grated lime zest

1 teaspoon coriander seeds

1 teaspoon cumin seeds

5 black peppercorns

1 teaspoon paprika

¼ teaspoon turmeric

¼ cup (2 fl oz/60 ml) light olive oil

1 medium yellow (brown) onion, chopped

1 lb (500 g) blade, round or chuck steak, cut into
   1 in (2.5 cm) cubes

6 cups (48 fl oz/1.5 L) beef pho stock (see page 11)

2 cups (16 fl oz/500 ml) coconut milk

4 medium-sized ripe tomatoes, chopped

2 teaspoons fish sauce

9 oz (280 g) shredded white or Chinese cabbage

Place chili pepper, shallots, garlic, galangal, cilantro, lime zest, coriander seeds, cumin seeds, peppercorns, paprika, turmeric and oil in a food processor and process to a smooth paste, about 2 minutes.

Place paste in a large saucepan over medium–low heat and cook, stirring, for 5 minutes. Add a little more oil if mixture starts to stick to bottom of pan. Add onion and meat, and cook, stirring, until onion is soft and meat is slightly browned, about 5 minutes.

Add stock, coconut milk, tomatoes and fish sauce, increase heat to medium and bring mixture to a steady simmer. Simmer until meat is tender, about 1½ hours.

Stir in cabbage and cook until cabbage is soft, about 10 minutes.

Ladle into individual bowls and serve.

Serves 4

Beef soup with ginger and asparagus

¼ cup (2 oz/60 g) miso paste

6 cups (48 fl oz/1.5 L) beef stock (see page 11) or water

2 in (5 cm) piece fresh ginger, peeled and cut into
thin strips

4 very small red onions, peeled and halved,
or 4 pearl onions

13 oz (400 g) beef fillet, cut into very thin slices

8 asparagus spears, thinly sliced crosswise

3 oz (90 g) very thinly sliced red cabbage

Place miso paste in a large saucepan with stock or water. Stir over medium–high heat until miso paste dissolves, 2–3 minutes. Allow liquid to come to a steady simmer. Add ginger (reserving a small amount for garnish) and onions and simmer for 10 minutes.

Add beef, asparagus and red cabbage and simmer until asparagus and cabbage are tender, 1–2 minutes.

Serve immediately, garnished with reserved ginger strips.

Serves 4

Variation

Instead of asparagus, use baby English spinach or finely sliced snow peas (mange-tout). For a spicier flavor, add chili sauce to taste.

Marinated beef laksa

10 oz (300 g) lean beef fillet

3 tablespoons lime juice

3 tablespoons light olive oil

1 teaspoon chili oil

1 small red chili pepper, chopped

2 scallions (shallots/spring onions), white part only,
    finely chopped

1 clove garlic, crushed

2 tablespoons finely chopped cilantro (fresh coriander)

¼ cup (2 oz/60 g) laksa paste (see page 13)

4 cups (32 fl oz/1 L) beef, beef pho or vegetable stock
    (see page 11)

4 cups (32 fl oz/1 L) coconut milk

2 teaspoons fish sauce

4 oz (125 g) baby English spinach leaves

4 oz (125 g) mixed fresh mushrooms, sliced if large,
    for garnish

4 oz (125 g) deep-fried tofu (about 4 pillows), sliced,
    for garnish

4 large sprigs cilantro (fresh coriander), for garnish

¼ cup (2 oz/60 g) crispy fried shallots (French shallots),
    for garnish (see page 92)

Wrap beef fillet in plastic wrap and freeze until partially
frozen, about 1 hour. Remove from freezer and slice into
very thin strips. Place in a ceramic or glass bowl and
add 1 tablespoon lime juice, 1 tablespoon olive oil, chili
oil, chili pepper, scallions, garlic and finely chopped
cilantro. Mix gently to combine marinade ingredients.
Cover and refrigerate for 1 hour.

Heat remaining oil in a large saucepan over
medium–high heat until hot, about 1 minute. Add laksa
paste and cook, stirring, until very fragrant, about
5 minutes. Add remaining lime juice, stock, coconut milk
and fish sauce, reduce heat to medium and bring
mixture to a steady simmer. Simmer for 15 minutes. Stir
in spinach and simmer until leaves have wilted, about
1 minute.

Remove beef from refrigerator. Ladle soup into
individual bowls and add beef and marinade. Top with
garnishes, finishing with crispy fried onions. The beef
and mushrooms will cook in the stock. Serve
immediately.

Serves 4

Beef with coconut milk and Thai herbs

2 cloves garlic

2 tablespoons peeled and finely chopped fresh ginger

3 shallots (French shallots), peeled

1 teaspoon galangal powder

½ teaspoon sea salt

½ teaspoon white peppercorns

4 cilantro (fresh coriander) roots

1 small red chili pepper

3 tablespoons light olive oil

12 oz (375 g) round or rump steak, cut into
    1 in (2.5 cm) cubes

5 cups (40 fl oz/1.25 L) coconut milk

3 cups (24 fl oz/750 ml) beef pho stock (see page 11)

2–3 tablespoons lemon juice

2 stalks lemongrass, bottom 4 in (10 cm) only, cut into
    2 in (5 cm) pieces

3 fresh or 6 dried kaffir lime leaves

2 teaspoons palm sugar or dark brown sugar

1 tablespoon fish sauce

6½ oz (200 g) baby English spinach leaves

Place garlic, ginger, shallots, galangal, salt, peppercorns, cilantro, chili pepper and 2 tablespoons oil in a food processor and process to a smooth paste, 1–2 minutes.

Heat remaining oil in a large saucepan over medium heat. Add paste and cook, stirring, until fragrant, 3–4 minutes. Add meat and cook for 3–4 minutes, turning to coat meat and brown it slightly. Add coconut milk, stock and lemon juice and bring mixture to a steady simmer. Add lemongrass, kaffir lime leaves, palm sugar and fish sauce and simmer until meat is tender, about 30 minutes.

Remove lemongrass and lime leaves. Season to taste with extra fish sauce if soup is not salty enough, or lemon juice if it is not tangy enough.

Stir in spinach leaves and let soup stand until leaves are wilted, about 1 minute. Serve immediately.

Serves 4

Hearty potato and salami soup

7 oz (220 g) spicy salami, finely diced

1 tablespoon olive oil

1 large yellow (brown) onion, chopped

2 cloves garlic, crushed

2 lb (1 kg) potatoes, peeled and cut into ¾ in (2 cm)
   cubes

1 medium carrot, peeled and chopped

6 cups (48 fl oz/1.5 L) chicken stock

1 bunch fresh baby English spinach, stemmed and
   shredded

Cook salami in a dry frying pan over medium–high heat
until browned. Drain on paper towels.

   Heat oil in same pan over medium heat. Add onion
and garlic and cook, stirring, until onion is soft. Add
potato, carrot and stock. Simmer, uncovered, until
vegetables are tender, 10–15 minutes.

   Add spinach, and stir over heat until wilted. Stir in
salami and serve.

Serves 4

Smoked ham minestrone

8 oz (250 g) small pasta shells

¼ cup (2 fl oz/60 ml) olive oil

8 oz (250 g) carrots, diced

8 oz (250 g) onions, chopped

2 cloves garlic, crushed

2 sticks celery, chopped

8 oz (250 g) zucchini (courgettes), diced

4 oz (125 g) smoked ham, diced

2–3 cups (16–24 fl oz/500–750 ml) vegetable stock
   (see page 11)

1 can (13 oz/400 g) cannellini beans, rinsed and drained

8 oz (250 g) broccoli florets

8 oz (250 g) green beans, sliced

¼ cup (2 fl oz/60 ml) prepared pesto, for serving

FOR PESTO

1 cup (1½ oz/45 g) well-packed basil leaves

2 oz (60 g) pine nuts, toasted

2 cloves garlic, chopped

pinch sea salt

juice of 1 lemon

2 oz (60 g) grated parmesan

½ cup (4 fl oz/125 ml) extra virgin olive oil

To make pesto: Place basil, pinenuts, garlic, salt, lemon juice and parmesan in a food processor or blender and puree. With motor running, gradually add oil and process until pesto has the consistency of thick paste. Store in an airtight container in the refrigerator for up to 3 weeks. Makes 1 cup (8 fl oz/250 ml).

Half-cook pasta in boiling salted water for 5 minutes, then drain.

Heat oil in a large saucepan over medium heat. Add onion, garlic and celery and cook, stirring, until onion is soft, about 5 minutes. Add zucchini and ham, and just enough stock to cover. Bring to a boil, then reduce heat and simmer until vegetables are just tender, about 10 minutes. Add cannellini beans and cook for 5 minutes. Stir in broccoli and green beans and simmer a further 5 minutes. Stir in half-cooked pasta and simmer until tender, about 5 minutes.

Serve soup with a dollop of pesto swirled through.

Serves 4

Red lentil, potato and ham soup

1½ cups (8 oz/250 g) red lentils
6¼ cups (50 fl oz/1.5 L) vegetable stock (see page 11)
   or water
1 ham bone or knuckle, or 6 oz (180 g) streaky bacon
   slices, rinded and chopped
1 large yellow (brown) onion, chopped
1 clove garlic, crushed
2 carrots, peeled and finely chopped or coarsely grated
3–4 tomatoes, peeled and chopped
1 bay leaf
salt and freshly ground black pepper, to taste
12 oz (375 g) potatoes, peeled and chopped
2 tablespoons wine vinegar
chopped fresh parsley, for garnish

FOR FRIED CROUTONS
3–4 slices bread (white or brown), crusts trimmed and
   cut into cubes
olive oil, for frying
garlic, halved (optional)

To make fried croutons: In a frying pan, heat about
1 in (2.5 cm) oil and garlic (if using). Add bread and fry,
turning as necessary, until golden brown, about
3–4 minutes. Discard garlic and drain croutons on paper
towels. Croutons can be stored in an airtight container
for up to 5 days.

Wash lentils and place in a large saucepan with stock
or water, ham bone or bacon, onion, garlic, carrot,
tomato, bay leaf and seasonings. Bring to a boil, remove
any scum from the surface, cover and simmer gently
until the lentils are tender, about 1 hour.

Discard bay leaf and remove ham bone, if using.
If preferred, the soup may be sieved or pureed at this
stage. Any trimmings may be removed from the ham
bone, finely chopped and returned to the soup.

Add potato and vinegar and simmer until potato is
tender, about 20 minutes.

Adjust the seasonings and serve very hot, sprinkled
liberally with chopped parsley and fried croutons.
Serves 6

Udon noodle soup with sesame pork and mushroom

7 oz (220 g) dried udon noodles

1 tablespoon peanut oil

1 x 2 in (5 cm) piece fresh ginger, peeled and grated

2 small leeks, white part only, thinly sliced

1 clove garlic, finely chopped

3 oz (90 g) fresh shiitake mushrooms, sliced

5 oz (150 g) button mushrooms, sliced

1 tablespoon soy sauce

1 tablespoon rice wine

6 cups (48 fl oz/1.5 L) chicken or beef stock
   (see pages 10 and 11)

2 teaspoons Asian sesame oil

12 oz (375 g) pork fillet

sea salt and ground white pepper, to taste

2 tablespoons finely chopped chives, for garnish

FOR FRIED ENOKI MUSHROOMS

¼ cup (2 oz/60 g) all-purpose (plain) flour

sea salt and freshly ground black pepper, to taste

1½ cups (12 fl oz/375 ml) peanut oil, for frying

4 bundles (2 oz/60 g) enoki mushrooms, divided into
   smaller bundles of 2 or 3 mushrooms

Bring a large pot of water to a boil. Add noodles and cook until tender, 7–9 minutes. Drain noodles, rinse with warm water and set aside.

Heat peanut oil in a saucepan over medium–high heat and add ginger, leeks, garlic and mushrooms and cook, stirring, until leeks and mushrooms are wilted, about 4–5 minutes. Add soy sauce, rice wine and stock, increase heat to high and bring liquid to a boil. Reduce heat to medium–low and simmer until ready to serve.

Heat sesame oil in a frying pan over high heat. Add pork fillet and cook, turning to brown all sides, about 4–7 minutes. Reduce heat to medium and continue to cook until pork is cooked through (test by cutting into thickest part), 4–5 minutes. Season to taste. Remove pork from pan and set aside for 5 minutes.

To make fried enoki mushrooms: In a small bowl, combine flour with salt and black pepper. Mix well. Heat peanut oil in a large saucepan over high heat until a drop of flour sizzles rapidly when dropped into oil. Coat mushrooms in flour, shaking off excess. Fry mushrooms in batches in hot oil until crisp and golden, about 40 seconds. Remove and drain on paper towels.

Cut pork into thin slices. Rinse noodles under very hot water, using a fork to separate them. Place noodles in individual bowls. Pour soup over noodles and top with pork slices and fried mushrooms. Sprinkle with chives and serve immediately.

Serves 4

Pork wonton asparagus and noodle soup

1 lb (500 g) fresh, white, rice noodles

12 oz (375 g) ground (minced) pork

½ teaspoon white pepper

½ teaspoon sea salt

1 tablespoon peeled and grated fresh ginger

2 cloves garlic, crushed

1 green chili pepper, finely chopped

16 wonton wrappers

10 oz (300 g) asparagus, trimmed

2 tablespoons soy sauce

1 tablespoon lemon juice

1 tablespoon toasted sesame seeds

freshly ground black pepper, to taste

8 cups (64 fl oz/2 L) chicken stock (see page 10)

1 tablespoon finely chopped cilantro (fresh coriander),
    for garnish

Bring a large pot of water to a boil, stir in noodles and cook until tender, 3–4 minutes. Drain noodles, rinse in very hot water and set aside. In a bowl, combine pork, salt, white pepper, ginger, garlic and chili pepper.

Lay wonton wrappers on a dry surface and place 1 heaping teaspoon of pork mixture in the center of each wrapper. Wet edges with a little water and fold in to form bundles, pressing edges together to secure filling.

Choose a large saucepan with a lid, and a large steamer, also with a lid – make sure the steamer and its lid will fit inside the covered saucepan. Pour boiling water into the saucepan to a depth of 1 in (2.5 cm). Cut a piece of waxed (greaseproof) paper (to fit bottom of steamer) and place in steamer. Arrange half the wontons on paper. Cover with steamer lid and place inside saucepan. Cover saucepan on and steam until wontons are tender, about 4 minutes. Set wontons aside on a slightly damp plate and cover with plastic wrap. Repeat with remaining wontons. Check water level in saucepan occasionally and add more if necessary.

Remove waxed (greaseproof) paper from steamer. Place asparagus spears in steamer. Cover and steam asparagus until tender, about 3 minutes. Place asparagus on a plate and drizzle with soy sauce and lemon juice. Sprinkle with sesame seeds and black pepper.

Place stock in a large saucepan and bring to a boil. Reduce heat to a steady simmer and add steamed wontons and cooked noodles. Simmer for 1 minute.

Ladle into individual bowls and serve topped with asparagus and sprinkled with cilantro.

Serves 4

Somen noodle, pork and scallion soup

8 oz (250 g) somen noodles

4 cups (32 fl oz/1 L) chicken stock (see page 10)

1 tablespoon dry sherry

1 tablespoon light soy sauce

6 scallions (shallots/spring onions), sliced

4 oz (125 g) Chinese barbecue pork, sliced

Asian chili oil, for serving (optional)

Cook noodles in boiling water until tender, about
3 minutes. Drain and divide among 4 individual bowls.

Place stock, sherry and soy sauce in saucepan. Bring
to boil. Reduce heat to low and simmer for 5 minutes.
Add scallions and pork. Cook for 1 minute.

Ladle soup over noodles. If using, serve with Asian
chili oil at the table, to be added to taste.

Serves 4

Seafood

Salmon rice soup

4 oz (125 g) salmon fillet, thickly sliced
½ teaspoon salt
4 cups (32 fl oz/1 L) water
1½ teaspoons instant dashi
4 cups (20 oz/600 g) cooked short-grain rice, heated
¼ teaspoon matcha powder
2 tablespoons wakame seaweed, soaked in warm water
   for 2 minutes
2 scallions (shallots/spring onions), thinly sliced
wasabi paste, for serving

Preheat broiler (grill). Place salmon slices in a single layer in a baking dish and sprinkle with salt. Broil (grill) salmon for about 2 minutes. Turn carefully with a spatula and cook on other side until almost cooked through, about 1 minute. Remove from heat.

Meanwhile, place water in a saucepan and bring to a boil. Add dashi and stir until well dissolved. Remove from heat.

Divide rice among 4 bowls, sprinkle with matcha powder and top with wakame and a slice of grilled salmon. Ladle soup to each bowl. Garnish with scallion slices and serve accompanied by wasabi.
Serves 4

Variation
Add spinach leaves to the water as it is brought to a boil, for a delicious alternative.

Hot and sour shrimp soup

12 oz (375 g) jumbo shrimp (king prawns)

3 cups (24 fl oz/750 ml) hot and sour stock (see page 13)

3 tablespoons coarsely chopped shallots (French shallots), preferably pink

2 firm tomatoes, each cut into 8 wedges

8 oz (250 g) fresh mushrooms, rinsed, drained and halved

5–10 whole small fresh green chili peppers

2–3 tablespoons fish sauce, to taste

5 fresh kaffir lime leaves, coarsely torn

2 tablespoons lime juice

½ cup (½ oz/15 g) coarsely chopped cilantro (fresh coriander) leaves and stems, for garnish

Peel and devein shrimp, leaving tails intact and reserving shells and heads for stock. Cover and refrigerate until ready to use.

In a medium saucepan, combine reserved shrimp heads and shells, and stock, and bring to a boil. Using a skimmer, remove and discard heads and shells. Bring back to a boil. Add shallots, tomatoes, mushrooms, chili peppers, fish sauce and kaffir lime leaves. Simmer gently for 2 minutes, then increase heat and bring soup back to a boil. Add shrimp, and rapidly boil for no more than 1 minute.

Remove soup from heat and stir in lime juice. Ladle soup into bowls, garnish with fresh cilantro, and serve.

Serves 4–6

Shrimp bisque

8 cups (64 fl oz/2 L) fish or seafood stock (see page 12)

2 lb (1 kg) uncooked shrimp (prawns), peeled and deveined

3 tablespoons butter

¼ cup (1 oz/30 g) all-purpose (plain) flour

1 cup (8 fl oz/250 ml) milk

2 tablespoons sherry

2 teaspoons chopped fresh chervil

2 teaspoons chopped fresh chives

2 teaspoons chopped fresh tarragon

salt and white pepper, to taste

Place stock in a large saucepan and bring to a boil. Add shrimp and simmer until no longer translucent, 3–5 minutes. Remove shrimp and reserve stock.

Place shrimp in a food processor with ¼ cup (2 fl oz/60 ml) reserved stock and process until smooth.

Melt butter in a large saucepan over medium heat. Add flour and cook for 1 minute. Remove from heat and gradually add remaining reserved stock and milk. Return to heat and bring to a boil, stirring constantly. Reduce heat and simmer until thick and creamy.

Add pureed shrimp, sherry, chervil, chives, tarragon, and salt and pepper. Serve immediately.

Serves 4

LEFT Hot and sour shrimp soup

Shrimp and onion soup

2 oz (60 g) butter
1 lb (500 g) yellow (brown) onions, sliced
4 cups (32 fl oz/1 L) fish or seafood stock (see page 12)
salt and freshly ground black pepper, to taste
1 lb (500 g) uncooked shrimp (prawns), peeled and
  deveined
4 oz (125 g) grated emmenthal cheese
6 slices French bread, toasted and buttered

Melt butter in a large saucepan over medium heat. Add onion and cook slowly over low heat until tender and golden, about 15 minutes.

Add stock and bring to a boil. Simmer for 15 minutes. Season with salt and pepper. Add shrimp, and cook just until shrimp are no longer translucent, 3–4 minutes.

Broil (grill) cheese onto bread. Place bread in soup bowls, pour soup over, and serve immediately.

Serves 6

Shrimp, tomato and chili soup

1 tablespoon olive oil
1 onion, sliced
2 cloves garlic, chopped
1 lb (500 g) uncooked shrimp (prawns), peeled (reserve
  shells) and deveined
3 cups (24 fl oz/750 ml) water
½ cup (4 fl oz/125 ml) dry white wine
2 tablespoons tomato paste
2–3 medium plum (Roma) tomatoes, peeled and
  chopped
1 chili pepper, seeded and chopped
¼ teaspoon salt
3 tablespoons chopped fresh basil

Heat olive oil in a large saucepan over medium heat. Add onion, garlic and reserved shrimp shells and sauté until onion is tender, about 4 minutes. Add water and wine and simmer for 15 minutes. Strain; reserve liquid and discard onion and shells.

Return stock to saucepan. Add tomato paste, tomatoes and chili pepper and bring to a boil over high heat. Reduce heat and simmer for 10 minutes.

Add shrimp, salt and basil and simmer until shrimp are no longer translucent, 3–4 minutes. Serve immediately.

Serves 4

RIGHT Shrimp and onion soup

Indian fish soup

1 tablespoon oil
1 onion, finely chopped
1 clove garlic, chopped
1 teaspoon peeled and chopped fresh ginger
1 teaspoon ground cumin
1 teaspoon ground coriander
4 cups (32 fl oz/1 L) fish stock (see page 12)
salt and freshly ground black pepper, to taste
½ cup (3 oz/90 g) uncooked long-grain rice
1 lb (500 g) white-fleshed fish fillets, cubed
2 tablespoons chopped cilantro (fresh coriander) leaves

Heat oil in a large saucepan over medium heat. Add onion and cook until tender, 3–4 minutes. Stir in garlic, ginger, cumin and coriander and cook until fragrant, about 1 minute.

Pour in stock, season with salt and pepper, and bring to a boil. Add rice and simmer until rice is tender, about 12 minutes.

Add fish and cilantro and simmer until fish is tender and beginning to flake when tested, 2–3 minutes. Serve immediately.

Serves 4

Mussels in spiced coconut milk broth

1 large yellow (brown) onion, sliced
3 cloves garlic
1 teaspoon ground coriander
¼ teaspoon turmeric
2 small red chili peppers
1 stalk lemongrass, bottom 3 in (7.5 cm) only, chopped
2 tablespoons lemon juice
1 tablespoon light olive oil
2 cups (16 fl oz/500 ml) fish stock (see page 12)
2 cups (16 fl oz/500 ml) coconut milk
2 teaspoons fish sauce
4 lb (2 kg) mussels in their shells, scrubbed
1 x 2 in (5 cm) piece fresh ginger, very finely sliced lengthwise and julienned
½ cup (½ oz/15 g) cilantro (fresh coriander) leaves

Place onion, garlic, coriander, turmeric, chili peppers, lemongrass and lemon juice in a food processor and process to a fine paste, 2–3 minutes.

Heat oil in a very large saucepan over medium heat Add paste and cook, stirring, until fragrant, about 5 minutes. Add fish stock, coconut milk and fish sauce, increase heat to high and bring liquid to a boil. Add mussels, then cover saucepan tightly and cook, shaking saucepan occasionally, until all mussels have opened, 7–8 minutes. Discard any mussels that do not open. Add ginger and cilantro and stir to combine thoroughly. Serve immediately in large bowls.

Serves 4

RIGHT Mussels in spiced coconut milk broth

Bouillabaisse

¼ cup (2 fl oz/60 ml) olive oil

1 yellow (brown) onion, chopped

1 clove garlic, chopped

¼ medium fennel bulb, chopped

4 cups (32 fl oz/1 L) fish or seafood stock (see page 12)

4–5 medium plum (Roma) tomatoes, peeled and chopped or 1 x 14 oz (440 g) can peeled tomatoes, chopped

¼ teaspoon turmeric

¼ teaspoon salt

¼ teaspoon freshly ground black pepper

4 small whole fish (such as garfish or red mullet), cleaned and scaled

1 lb (500 g) white-fleshed fish fillets, cut into pieces

1 lb (500 g) uncooked shrimp (prawns), peeled and deveined

1 lb (500 g) mussels, scrubbed and debearded

⅓ cup (½ oz/15 g) chopped fresh parsley

4 slices French bread, toasted

chopped fresh parsley, for serving

FOR GREEN AIOLI

2 eggs yolks

2 tablespoons lemon juice

salt and freshly ground black pepper, to taste

3 cloves garlic, chopped

2 tablespoons chopped fresh parsley

2 tablespoons chopped fresh chives

1 tablespoon chopped fresh tarragon

1 cup (8 fl oz/250 ml) olive oil

To make green aioli: Combine yolks, lemon juice, salt and pepper, garlic, parsley, chives, and tarragon in food processor or blender and mix until smooth. With motor running, gradually pour in oil until all is incorporated. Serve at room temperature, if possible.

Heat oil in large saucepan over medium heat. Add onion, garlic and fennel and cook until tender, 3–4 minutes. Add stock, tomatoes, turmeric, salt and pepper, bring to a boil and simmer for 15 minutes.

Add whole fish and simmer for 5 minutes. Add fish pieces and shrimp and simmer for 2 minutes. Add mussels and parsley and cook until mussels open, 2–3 minutes; discard any that do not open.

To serve, place French bread in soup bowls. Top with seafood and broth and spoon 1 tablespoon of aïoli on top. Sprinkle with extra parsley.

Serves 4

Seafood soup

¼ cup (2 fl oz/60 ml) olive oil

1 stalk celery, chopped

1 small carrot, peeled and chopped

1 yellow (brown) onion, finely chopped

3 cloves garlic, chopped

⅓ cup (½ oz/15 g) chopped fresh parsley

2 bay leaves

2–3 medium plum (Roma) tomatoes, peeled, seeded
   and chopped

½ cup (4 fl oz/125 ml) dry white wine

4 cups (32 fl oz/1 L) fish or seafood stock (see page 12)

⅓ cup (2 oz/60 g) uncooked short-grain rice

1 lb (500 g) white-fleshed or oily fish fillets, cubed

1 lb (500 g) mussels, scrubbed and debearded

Heat oil in a large saucepan over medium heat. Add
celery, carrot and onion and cook until tender, about
5 minutes.

   Add garlic, parsley, bay leaves, tomatoes, wine and
stock and simmer for 15 minutes.

   Add rice and simmer for 8 minutes, stirring
occasionally.

   Add fish and mussels and simmer until rice is tender
and mussels have opened, about 4 minutes; discard any
mussels that do not open. Serve immediately.

Serves 4–6

Clam chowder

14 oz (440 g) canned clams, undrained

2 rashers bacon, chopped

1 small yellow (brown) onion, chopped

3 large potatoes, peeled and diced

salt and white pepper, to taste

1½ cups (12 fl oz/375 ml) fish or seafood stock
(see page 12) or water

½ cup (4 fl oz/125 ml) light (single) cream

½ cup (4 fl oz/125 ml) milk

Remove clams from liquid; reserve 1½ cups (12 fl oz/375 ml) of the liquid. Chop clams into small chunks.

Fry bacon in a saucepan over low heat until crisp. Add onion and sauté over medium heat until soft. Add potato and toss through. Add salt and pepper, reserved clam liquid and stock or water. Simmer until potato is tender, about 15 minutes.

Add clams, cream and milk, and gently heat through.

Let stand, if possible (see below). Reheat if necessary and serve warm.

Serves 2–4

Hints

Chowder improves with standing, so if you have time, let it stand off the heat for 1 hour or refrigerate it overnight before reheating.

Serve topped with chopped fresh chives or thyme and freshly ground black pepper.

Salted crackers are the traditional accompaniment.

You may like to add a handful of finely chopped celery, green bell pepper (capsicum) and/or carrot with the potatoes.

Corn chowder can be made by using canned corn kernels instead of clams, and vegetable or chicken stock instead of fish stock.

Fennel and oyster soup

2 tablespoons (1 oz/30 g) butter
1 yellow (brown) onion, chopped
½ medium fennel bulb, chopped
1 teaspoon fennel seeds
3 cups (24 fl oz/750 ml) fish or seafood stock
   (see page 12)
2 dozen oysters on the half shell or 1 small jar oysters,
   drained
½ cup (4 fl oz/125 ml) light (single) cream
salt and freshly ground black pepper, to taste

Melt butter in a saucepan over medium heat. Add onion,
fennel and fennel seeds and cook until vegetables are
tender, about 5 minutes. Pour in stock and simmer for
15 minutes.

   Pure mixture in a food processor. Return puree to
saucepan and stir through cream. Season with salt and
pepper. Bring just to a boil, add oysters (without shells)
and warm through. Serve hot.

Serves 4

Scallop and potato soup

2 tablespoons olive oil
1 medium leek, trimmed, washed and sliced thinly
1 medium potato, peeled and finely chopped
1 stalk celery, finely chopped
1 medium carrot, peeled and finely chopped
1 cup (8 oz/250 ml) tomato puree
4 cups (32 fl oz/1 L) fish or seafood stock (see page 12)
1 lb (500 g) scallops, deveined
3 tablespoons finely chopped fresh chives
salt and freshly ground black pepper, to taste

Heat olive oil in a large saucepan over medium heat. Add leek, potato, celery and carrot and cook until tender, about 10 minutes.

Add tomato puree and stock and bring to a boil. Reduce heat and simmer for 15 minutes.

Add scallops, chives and salt and pepper, and simmer until scallops are tender, 1–2 minutes. Serve immediately.

Serves 4

Scallop and leek soup

2 tablespoons butter
1 medium leek
2 cloves garlic, chopped
½ cup (4 fl oz/125 ml) milk
1 egg yolk, beaten
2 cups (16 fl oz/500 ml) fish stock (see page 12)
8 oz (250 g) scallops, deveined
2 tablespoons chopped fresh dill
salt and freshly ground black pepper, to taste

Trim root and green section from leek and discard. Slice white portion and rinse under cold running water to remove all dirt.

Melt butter in medium saucepan over medium heat. Add leek and garlic and cook until tender, about 3 minutes.

Whisk together milk and egg yolk. Pour milk mixture into saucepan with stock, bring to a boil and stir until thickened.

Add scallops, dill and salt and pepper and simmer until scallops are tender.

Serves 4

Poached salmon and green bean soup

1 tablespoon light olive oil

1 medium yellow (brown) onion, finely diced

1 small red chili pepper, finely chopped

3 stalks lemongrass, bottom 3 in (7.5 cm) only,
    cut lengthwise in half

4 fresh or 8 dried kaffir lime leaves

3 cups (24 fl oz/750 ml) fish stock (see page 12)

3 cups (24 fl oz/750 ml) coconut milk

3 tablespoons lime juice

2 teaspoons fish sauce

freshly ground black or white pepper, to taste

1 lb (500 g) salmon fillet, skin and any bones removed,
    cut into 1 in (2.5 cm) pieces

10 oz (310 g) fava (broad) beans, peeled

8 oz (250 g) baby green beans, trimmed (and halved
    if large)

Heat olive oil in a large saucepan over medium heat. Add onion and chili pepper and cook, stirring, until onion is soft, 4–5 minutes. Add lemongrass, kaffir lime leaves, stock, coconut milk, lime juice, fish sauce and ground pepper. Bring liquid to a steady simmer. Simmer for 15 minutes.

Reduce heat to medium–low and add salmon. Cook for 2 minutes, then add fava and green beans and cook until beans are just tender and salmon is just cooked through, 3–4 minutes. Add more fish sauce if soup is not salty enough, more lime juice if it is not tangy enough. Serve immediately.

Serves 4

Crab and asparagus soup

2 lb (1 kg) raw or cooked crab in its shell, or 1 lb (500 g)
   prepared crabmeat
25 dried black mushrooms
6 cups (48 fl oz/1.5 L) water, or, if using precooked
   crab, fish or seafood stock (see page 12)
6 spears asparagus, trimmed
1 tablespoon arrowroot or cornstarch (cornflour)
   dissolved in 1 tablespoon water
1 teaspoon salt, or to taste
½ teaspoon freshly ground black pepper, or to taste
1 egg white
⅓ cup (½ oz/15 g) coarsely torn fresh cilantro (fresh
   coriander) sprigs, for garnish

If using raw crabs, scrub them with a scouring brush under cold running water, then plunge them into a deep pot of lightly salted boiling water—about 6 cups (48 fl oz/1.5 L). Cook for 10–15 minutes, depending on size. Remove crabs with a slotted spoon, reserving cooking liquid. Clean crabs by pulling off apron flap from under shell. Pry off top shell and rinse away breathing ducts or lungs. Break or cut body in half, or cut large crabs into smaller pieces. Twist off claws, reserving pincers for garnish. Refrigerate until ready to use.

Soak mushrooms in hot water for about 20 minutes, then drain, squeezing to remove all liquid. Use shears or a small knife to cut away tough stems. Discard stems. Cut mushroom caps into thin julienne, then crosswise into small dice; set aside.

In a large pot, bring 6 cups (48 fl oz/1.5 L) reserved liquid from cooking crab, or stock if using precooked crab, to a boil.

Peel asparagus, then cut off about 1½ in (4 cm) of tips and set them aside. Chop remaining asparagus into thin rounds. Add asparagus tips to boiling liquid and cook for 2 minutes. Using a slotted spoon, transfer asparagus tips to a bowl. Whisk arrowroot and water mixture into soup. Add sliced asparagus. Bring to a gentle boil to thicken. Season with salt and pepper. Whisk in egg white.

At the last minute, add crabmeat and mushrooms. Stir to combine, then remove from heat. To serve, garnish with cilantro sprigs and reserved asparagus tips.
Serves 6

Sour crabmeat soup

1 tablespoon light olive oil
2 medium red onions, sliced
1 x 2 in (5 cm) piece fresh ginger, peeled and sliced
4 cloves garlic, crushed
2 stalks lemongrass, bottom 3 in (7.5 cm) only,
    cut lengthwise into strips
1 small red chili pepper, finely chopped
3 tablespoons lime juice
3 fresh or 6 dried kaffir lime leaves
8 cups (64 fl oz/2 L) fish stock (see page 12)
2 teaspoons fish sauce
1 lb (500 g) prepared crabmeat
1 small red onion, very thinly sliced, for garnish
1 red chili pepper, sliced crosswise, for garnish

Heat oil in a large saucepan over medium–high heat.
Add sliced onions and cook until they begin to soften,
about 3 minutes. Add ginger, garlic, lemongrass and chili
pepper and cook, stirring, until mixture is fragrant, about
3 minutes. Add lime juice, kaffir lime leaves, stock and
fish sauce and bring mixture to a steady simmer. Simmer
for 20 minutes.

   Strain mixture through a fine sieve, discarding solids,
and return liquid to saucepan. Heat over medium heat
until it simmers, 2–3 minutes. Add crabmeat and simmer
until heated through, 2–3 minutes.

   Pour into individual bowls and serve immediately,
garnished with thin slices of onion and chili pepper.
Serves 4

Coconut-shrimp soup

1 lb (500 g) jumbo shrimp (king prawns), peeled and deveined (reserve heads and shells)

1 stalk lemongrass, chopped, or 2 teaspoons grated lemon zest

1 carrot, peeled and sliced

1 stick celery, sliced

1 yellow (brown) onion, sliced

2 plum (Roma) tomatoes, chopped

1 bunch cilantro (fresh coriander)

6 cups (48 fl oz/1.5 L) water

2 cups (16 fl oz/500 ml) coconut milk

1½ tablespoons red curry paste

1 teaspoon palm sugar or brown sugar

2 teaspoons fish sauce

8 oz (250 g) hokkien noodles

juice of 2 limes

Place reserved shrimp heads and shells in a large saucepan. Add lemongrass or lemon zest, carrot, celery, onion and tomatoes. Remove cilantro leaves from stems. Chop stems and add to saucepan; chop leaves and reserve. Add water to pan. Bring to a boil, reduce heat to low, cover and simmer gently, stirring occasionally, for 20 minutes. Strain through fine-mesh sieve. Reserve 5 cups (40 fl oz/1.25 L) stock.

Return reserved stock to saucepan. Stir in coconut milk, curry paste, sugar, fish sauce, noodles, lime juice, cilantro leaves and shrimp. Bring to a boil, reduce heat to low, cover and simmer, stirring occasionally, until shrimp are no longer translucent, 6–7 minutes.

Ladle into individual bowls and serve.

Serves 4

Seafood laksa

1½ tablespoons light olive oil

½ cup (4 oz/125 g) laksa paste (see page 13)

2 tablespoons lime or lemon juice

3 cups (24 fl oz/750 ml) coconut milk

3 cups (24 fl oz/750 ml) fish or seafood stock
   (see page 12)

6 oz (180 g) dried rice vermicelli noodles

12 oz (375 g) medium shrimp (prawns), peeled and
   deveined, tails left intact

1 lb (500 g) salmon fillet, cut into 8 pieces, each
   1 in (5 cm) thick

1 medium red onion, thinly sliced

1 medium cucumber, peeled and sliced

7 oz (220 g) bean sprouts, trimmed

5 oz (150 g) mustard cress shoots
   or snow pea (mange-tout) shoots

1 medium mango, peeled, seeded and diced

2 tablespoons small mint leaves

FOR CRISPY FRIED SHALLOTS

2 cups (16 fl oz/500 ml) peanut oil

5 or 6 medium shallots (French shallots), about
   5 oz (150 g), peeled and very thinly sliced

To make laksa: Heat oil in a large saucepan over medium–high heat. Stir in laksa paste and cook, stirring, until fragrant, 4–5 minutes. Add lime or lemon juice, coconut milk and stock and stir until thoroughly combined. Reduce heat to medium and simmer for 10 minutes.

Place noodles in a large bowl and add boiling water to cover. Let stand until noodles are soft, 3–4 minutes. Drain noodles, rinse under warm water and set aside.

Add shrimp and salmon to soup and simmer until shrimp are cooked through and salmon is just cooked through, 3–4 minutes.

To make crispy fried shallots: Heat oil in a medium saucepan over high heat until it reaches 375°F (190°C) on a deep-frying thermometer. Add shallots all at once and fry until golden, about 1½ minutes. Remove with a slotted spoon and drain on a plate lined with paper towels. Reserve ¼ cup for garnish and store remaining crispy fried shallots in an airtight container for later use.

Rinse noodles under very hot water, using a fork to separate them.

Spoon noodles into individual bowls and top with soup and seafood. Top with onion, cucumber, bean sprouts, mustard cress shoots, mango, mint leaves, finishing with crispy fried shallots. Serve immediately.
Serves 4

Miso with tuna and ginger

½ lb (250 g) white-fleshed fish fillet

2 teaspoons Asian chili oil

1 small red chili pepper, finely chopped

2 cloves garlic, crushed

1 x 2 in (5 cm) piece fresh ginger, peeled and finely
    grated

1 medium red onion, very finely sliced

½ teaspoon white pepper

3 tablespoons lime juice

2 teaspoons fish sauce

3 medium tomatoes, cored and chopped into
    ¾ in (2 cm) pieces

6 oz (180 g) thin rice noodles

6 cups (48 fl oz/1.5 L) fish stock (see page 12)

4 sprigs cilantro (fresh coriander), for garnish

Remove skin and any bones from fish fillet and cut fish
diagonally, across grain, into very thin slices. Place in a
large glass or ceramic bowl and add chili oil, chili
pepper, garlic, ginger, onion, white pepper, lime juice,
fish sauce and tomatoes. Stir very gently to coat fish
with marinade. Cover with plastic wrap and refrigerate
for 2–3 hours.

Place noodles in a bowl and add boiling water to
cover. Let noodles stand until soft, 3–4 minutes. Drain
noodles, rinse under warm water and set aside.

When ready to serve, rinse noodles under very hot
water, using a fork to separate them. Drain and divide
among bowls. Spoon fish mixture over noodles.

Bring stock to a boil over high heat. Immediately pour
into bowls so ingredients are completely covered. Let
soup stand until fish is cooked, 3–4 minutes. Serve
garnished with cilantro sprigs.

Serves 4

Marinated shrimp, noodle and herb soup

2 lb (1 kg) shrimp (prawns), peeled, heads and shells
   reserved
2 tablespoons soy sauce
2 tablespoons lemon juice
1 large yellow (brown) onion, chopped
1 x 2 in (5 cm) piece fresh ginger, peeled and sliced
4 fresh or 8 dried kaffir lime leaves
2 stalks lemongrass, cut lengthwise into 3 in (7.5 cm)
   lengths, or 4 strips lemon zest
sea salt, to taste
8 oz (250 g) fresh egg noodles
½ cup (½ oz/15 g) cilantro (fresh coriander) leaves

½ cup (½ oz/15 g) small basil leaves
8 oz (250 g) Asian greens such as bok choy
   or choy sum, or English spinach, chopped
4 scallions (shallots/spring onions), thinly sliced,
   for garnish

Place shrimp in a glass or ceramic bowl and add soy
sauce and lemon juice. Stir so that shrimp are
thoroughly covered with the marinade. Cover and
refrigerate for at least 30 minutes.

Place shrimp heads and shells in a large saucepan
with onion, ginger, kaffir lime leaves and lemongrass.
Add 8 cups (64 fl oz/2 L) water, place over medium–high
heat and bring to a steady simmer. Simmer for
25 minutes. Add salt. Strain and reserve broth. Discard
solids.

Bring a large pot of water to a boil. Add noodles and
cook until soft and cooked through, 5–7 minutes. Drain
noodles, then rinse under very hot water and set aside.

Skim shrimp stock of any residue on surface and
place in a large saucepan over medium–high heat. Bring
to a steady simmer, then add noodles and shrimp and
marinade. Reduce heat to low and simmer until heated
through, about 1 minute. Add herbs and chopped
greens and simmer until greens have wilted, about
1 minute.

Ladle into individual bowls and serve topped with
sliced scallions.

Serves 4

Marinated lime-and-chili fish soup

8 oz (250 g) white-fleshed fish fillet

2 teaspoons Asian chili oil

1 small red chili pepper, finely chopped

2 cloves garlic, crushed

1 x 2 in (5 cm) piece fresh ginger, peeled and
   finely grated

1 medium red (Spanish) onion, very finely sliced

½ teaspoon white pepper

3 tablespoons lime juice

2 teaspoons fish sauce

3 medium tomatoes, cored and chopped into
   ¾ in (2 cm) pieces

6 oz (180 g) thin rice noodles

6 cups (48 fl oz/1.5 L) fish stock (see page 12)

4 sprigs cilantro (fresh coriander), for garnish

Remove skin and any bones from fish fillet and cut fish diagonally, across grain, into very thin slices. Place in a large glass or ceramic bowl and add chili oil, chili pepper, garlic, ginger, onion, white pepper, lime juice, fish sauce and tomatoes. Stir very gently to coat fish with marinade. Cover with plastic wrap and refrigerate for 2–3 hours.

Place noodles in a bowl and add boiling water to cover. Let noodles stand until soft, 3–4 minutes. Drain noodles, rinse under warm water and set aside.

When ready to serve, rinse noodles under very hot water, using a fork to separate them. Drain and divide among bowls. Spoon fish mixture over noodles. Bring stock to a boil over high heat. Immediately pour into bowls so ingredients are completely covered. Let soup stand until fish is cooked, 3–4 minutes. Serve garnished with cilantro sprigs.

Serves 4

Vegetable

Tofu and vegetable soup

2 cups (16 fl oz/500 ml) water
1 sheet dried seaweed (kombu), about
    4 in (10 cm) square
3 oz (90 g) dried anchovies (ikan bilis)
6 oz (180 g) firm tofu
1 daepa or scallion (shallot/spring onion)
1 red chili pepper
1 green chili pepper
1 small zucchini (courgette)
4 tablespoons soybean paste
4 teaspoons hot red chili paste
3–4 cloves garlic, crushed
steamed rice, for serving

Bring 2 cups (16 fl oz/500 ml) water to a boil in a saucepan. Add seaweed and anchovies, and boil for 15–20 minutes to make a stock.

Meanwhile, cut tofu into pieces ½ in (1 cm) thick, slice daepa and red and green chili peppers diagonally into pieces 1⁄16 in (2 mm) thick, and cut zucchini in half lengthwise, then into half-moon slices.

Add soybean paste and red chili paste to stock and stir to dissolve. Add garlic to stock, then tofu, daepa and zucchini. Reduce heat to medium and cook for 5 minutes, then add chili peppers.

Ladle into individual bowls and serve hot with steamed rice.

Serves 4

Variation
Add 1 oz (30 g) stewing (gravy) beef, sliced thinly into 1½ in (4 cm) strips, to the stock with the garlic.

Pea, potato, leek and tofu soup

2 tablespoons olive oil

1 clove garlic, finely chopped

2 medium leeks (white part only), rinsed and thinly
   sliced

1 lb (500 g) potatoes, peeled and diced

6 cups (48 fl oz/1.5 L) chicken or vegetable stock
   (see pages 10 and 11)

¼ teaspoon salt

8 oz (250 g) fresh or frozen peas

5 oz (150 g) silken firm or silken soft tofu, drained

cracked black pepper, to taste, for garnish

2 tablespoons finely chopped fresh parsley, for garnish

fried tempeh strips, for garnish (optional)

In a large saucepan, heat oil over medium heat. Sauté
garlic and leek until soft and just beginning to brown,
about 5 minutes. Add potato, stock and salt, cover and
simmer until potato is cooked through, about 8 minutes.
Add peas and simmer for 5–6 minutes.

   Remove from heat, place in a blender and puree in
batches with tofu until smooth. Return to heat and
warm, if serving hot; otherwise, refrigerate and serve
chilled.

   To serve, garnish with black pepper, parsley and fried
strips of tempeh, if using.

Serves 4–6

Sweet potato, chili and coconut soup

2 lb (1 kg) orange-fleshed sweet potatoes, peeled
   and diced

4 cups (32 fl oz/1 L) vegetable stock (see page 10)

1 cup (8 fl oz/250 ml) coconut milk or cream

1–2 small red chili peppers, seeded and sliced into thin
   strips

salt and freshly ground black pepper, to taste

chopped cilantro (fresh coriander), for garnish

Place sweet potato and stock in a large saucepan and
bring to a boil. Cover and simmer until tender, about
30 minutes.

   Transfer to a food processor and puree until smooth.
Return to saucepan and stir in coconut milk or cream
and chili pepper. Season with salt and pepper and serve
garnished with fresh cilantro.

Serves 4

LEFT Pea, potato, leek and tofu soup

Spicy tomato and cauliflower soup

1 teaspoon coriander seeds
1 teaspoon cumin seeds
1 tablespoon vegetable oil
1 large yellow (brown) onion, chopped
1 teaspoon ground turmeric
½ teaspoon cayenne pepper
1 cauliflower, trimmed and cut into florets
12 oz (375 g) potatoes, peeled and cubed
8–10 medium tomatoes, peeled and chopped
4 cups (32 fl oz/1 L) vegetable stock (see page 11)
salt and freshly ground black pepper, to taste
6 tablespoons plain (natural) yogurt or crème fraîche,
    for garnish (optional)

Dry-fry coriander and cumin seeds in a nonstick frying
pan until fragrant, about 1 minute. Transfer to a pestle
and mortar or spice grinder and grind to a powder.

Heat vegetable oil in a large saucepan and fry onion,
stirring, until soft, about 5 minutes. Add ground spice
mixture, turmeric and cayenne and fry, stirring, for
1 minute.

Add cauliflower, potato, tomatoes and stock and
bring to a boil. Cover and simmer until vegetables are
tender, about 30 minutes.

Transfer to a food processor and puree until smooth.
Season to taste and serve garnished with a tablespoon
of yogurt or crème fraîche in each bowl if using.
Serves 6

Curried cauliflower soup

2 tablespoons vegetable oil
1 clove garlic, crushed
1 medium leek, trimmed, washed and sliced
1 lb (500 g) cauliflower florets
2 sticks celery, sliced
1 tablespoon Thai red curry paste
2½ cups (20 fl oz/625 ml) vegetable stock (see page 11)
1 cup (8 fl oz/250 ml) thick coconut cream
1 x 10 oz (300 g) can lima (butter) or cannellini beans,
    drained
sea salt and freshly ground black pepper, to taste
celery leaves, for garnish
¼ cup (¼ oz/7 g) whole cilantro (fresh coriander)
    leaves, for garnish

Warm oil in a large saucepan over medium heat. When
oil is hot but not smoking, add garlic, leek, cauliflower
and celery and cook, stirring, over medium heat, for
5 minutes. Stir in curry paste and stock and cook,
increasing heat if necessary, until mixture is at a steady
simmer. Cover and allow to simmer until cauliflower is
tender, about 10 minutes.

Add coconut cream, beans, and salt and pepper.
Heat soup through, about 3 minutes, but do not allow it
to boil. Ladle soup into serving bowls and garnish with
celery and cilantro leaves.
Serves 4

RIGHT Curried cauliflower soup

Chunky vegetable soup

1 tablespoon olive oil

2 large onions, chopped

2 cloves garlic, chopped

1 stick celery, chopped

3 cups (24 fl oz/750 ml) tomato or mixed vegetable juice

3 cups (24 fl oz/750 ml) chicken or vegetable stock (see pages 10 and 11)

6 unpeeled small new potatoes, cut into 1 in (2.5 cm) chunks

8 oz (250 g) young turnips, cut into 1 in (2.5 cm) chunks

1 lb (500 g) carrots or young parsnips, or a combination, peeled and cut into ½ in (1 cm) cubes

4 unpeeled zucchini (courgettes), halved or quartered lengthwise and thickly sliced

6–8 small yellow squash, halved and thickly sliced

2 oz (60 g) fresh or frozen peas or whole corn kernels

2–3 sprigs fresh parsley, chopped

2 tablespoons chopped fresh basil or 1 teaspoon dried basil

freshly ground black pepper, to taste

crusty bread, for serving

Heat olive oil in a large heavy-based saucepan over medium heat and cook onion, garlic and celery, stirring, until golden, about 5 minutes. Add juice and stock to pan and bring to a boil.

Add potatoes and turnips to pan. Reduce heat and simmer until vegetables are almost tender, 12–15 minutes.

Add carrots or parsnips, zucchini, squash, peas, parsley, basil and pepper to pan. Simmer, stirring occasionally, until vegetables are tender, about 10 minutes.

Serve in heated deep soup plates with crusty bread.

Serves 4–6

Peasant bean soup

1 tablespoon olive oil

2 cloves garlic, chopped

1 large yellow (brown) onion, chopped

1 x 14 oz (440 g) can peeled tomatoes, undrained

1 x 13 oz (400 g) can borlotti beans

4 cups (32 fl oz/1 L) chicken or vegetable stock
   (see pages 10 and 11)

¼ cup (2 oz/60 g) tomato paste

1 teaspoon dried thyme or 2 teaspoons fresh thyme

1 teaspoon dried basil or 1 tablespoon fresh basil

1 bay leaf

4 oz (125 g) broken spaghetti or macaroni

Place olive oil, garlic and onion in a deep, heavy-based saucepan and cook over medium heat until onion is soft. Add tomatoes with juice, break up roughly, and cook for a couple of minutes.

Add beans, stock, tomato paste, thyme, basil and bay leaf and simmer gently for 10 minutes. Add pasta and simmer until soft, 5–10 minutes.

Serves 4

Variations

Substitute red kidney beans, cannellini or mixed beans.

Add chopped bacon with the onions.

Instead of beans and pasta, mash 1 large potato and stir it through the soup.

Country vegetable soup with pasta

1 tablespoon olive oil

1 onion, chopped

1 clove garlic, crushed

1 large leek, trimmed, washed and sliced

2 medium carrots, sliced

5 cups (40 fl oz/1.25 L) vegetable stock (see page 11)

4-5 medium plum (Roma) tomatoes, peeled and diced
   or 1 x 14 oz (440 g) can chopped tomatoes

2 medium zucchini (courgettes), sliced

6 oz (180 g) cabbage, shredded

4 oz (125 g) green beans, ends removed

4 oz (125 g) macaroni

salt and freshly ground black pepper, to taste

¼ cup (4 oz/125 g) pesto (see page 66)

Heat olive oil in a large saucepan. Add onion, garlic and leek and cook until soft. Add carrots, stock and tomatoes with their juice. Bring to a boil, then reduce heat, cover, and simmer for 30 minutes.

Add zucchini, cabbage, beans and macaroni to pan, and season. Simmer, covered, until macaroni is tender, 10–15 minutes.

Serve soup immediately, topped with a little pesto.

Serves 6

Tomato soup

2 lb (1 kg) tomatoes, peeled
2 teaspoons extra virgin olive oil
2 cloves garlic, finely chopped
1 yellow (brown) onion, finely chopped
1 stick celery, finely chopped
4 cups (32 fl oz/1 L) vegetable stock (see page 11)
1 tablespoon tomato paste
½ teaspoon sugar
salt and freshly ground black pepper, to taste
1 bay leaf
1 tablespoon chopped fresh basil
1 tablespoon chopped fresh oregano
1 tablespoon chopped fresh parsley

Puree tomatoes in a food processor and pour into a
bowl through a sieve to remove seeds.

Heat olive oil and garlic in a saucepan over a medium
heat until fragrant, about 1 minute. Add onion and celery
and cook gently until soft. Add pureed tomatoes, stock,
tomato paste, sugar, salt and pepper and bay leaf.
Simmer gently for about 20 minutes.

Remove bay leaf and add basil, oregano and parsley.
Cook until slightly thickened, 5–10 minutes, and serve
immediately.

Serves 4

Spinach and lentil soup

1½ cups (10 oz/300 g) dried brown lentils
6 cups (48 fl oz/1.5L) cold water
1 bunch English spinach
¼ cup (2 fl oz/60 ml) olive oil
1 large yellow (brown) onion, finely chopped
3 cloves garlic, finely chopped
3 tablespoons chopped cilantro (fresh coriander)
salt and freshly ground black pepper, to taste
¼ cup (2 fl oz/60 ml) lemon juice
extra virgin olive oil, for serving
lemon wedges, for serving
pita or other bread, for serving

Rinse lentils well in a sieve under cold running water.
Place in a heavy-based saucepan with cold water. Bring
to a boil, then cover and simmer until lentils are tender,
25–30 minutes, skimming surface if necessary.

Wash spinach well, slit leaves down the middle, then
shred coarsely. In another heavy-based saucepan, warm
olive oil over medium–low heat. Add onion and fry gently
until translucent. Stir in garlic and cook for a few
seconds longer. Add shredded spinach to pan and fry,
stirring often, until leaves wilt.

Add onion and spinach to lentils, along with cilantro,
salt and pepper, and lemon juice. Cover and simmer for
10 minutes more.

Serve soup in deep soup bowls with olive oil, lemon
wedges (for squeezing) and bread.

Serves 5–6

RIGHT Spinach and lentil soup

Vegetable and lentil soup

3 tablespoons peanut oil

2 tablespoons peeled and grated fresh ginger

1 small red chili pepper, seeded and finely sliced

¼ teaspoon ground cumin

¼ teaspoon curry powder

1 small red onion, chopped

1 small parsnip, peeled and sliced

2 sticks celery, thinly sliced

4 large carrots, peeled and sliced

1 potato, peeled and sliced

2 fresh kaffir lime leaves or ½ teaspoon grated
   lime zest

½ cup (3½ oz/100 g) red or brown lentils

6 cups (48 fl oz/1.5 L) vegetable stock or water
   (see page 11)

1 cup (8 fl oz/250 ml) coconut milk

2 tablespoons chopped cilantro (fresh coriander),
   for garnish

Heat peanut oil in a large saucepan over medium heat. Add ginger, chili pepper, cumin and curry powder and cook until aromatic, about 1 minute. Add onion, parsnip, celery, carrots, potato and kaffir lime leaves or lime zest. Cover and cook, stirring occasionally, for 10 minutes.

Add lentils and stock and bring to a boil. Cover and cook until vegetables and lentils are soft, about 20 minutes. Remove lime leaves and discard.

Working in batches, puree soup in a food processor. Return soup to pan, add coconut milk and heat through, about 3 minutes.

Ladle soup into individual bowls, garnish with chopped cilantro and serve immediately.

Serves 4

Vichysoisse with Thai herbs

4 leeks
2 oz (60 g) butter
1½ lb (750 g) potatoes, peeled and cubed
8 cups (64 fl oz/2 L) vegetable stock (see page 11)
    or water
sea salt and freshly ground black pepper, to taste
1 cup (8 fl oz/250 ml) coconut milk

FOR THAI HERBS
2 cloves garlic, chopped
¼ cup (¼ oz/7 g) loosely packed fresh flat-leaf (Italian)
    parsley leaves
¼ cup chopped cilantro (fresh coriander)
¼ small red chili pepper, seeded and chopped
grated zest of ½ lemon

Trim root and green section from leek and discard. Slice white portion and rinse under cold running water to remove all dirt.

Melt butter in a large saucepan over medium heat. Add leek and cook until softened, about 5 minutes.

Add potatoes and stock or water, cover and cook until potatoes are tender, about 30 minutes.

To make Thai herbs: In a bowl, combine garlic, parsley, cilantro, chili pepper and lemon zest and mix well. Set aside until ready to serve.

Working in batches, puree soup in a food processor. Return soup to saucepan and heat through, 3–5 minutes. Season with salt and pepper.

Ladle soup into bowls and swirl 2 tablespoons coconut milk into each serving. Garnish with a spoonful of Thai herbs.
Serves 6

Carrot and ginger soup

1 tablespoon vegetable oil

1 small red chili pepper, seeded and chopped

4 cloves garlic, crushed

3 teaspoons peeled and grated fresh ginger

2 onions, chopped

2 lb (1 kg) carrots, peeled and sliced

1 teaspoon ground cumin

1 teaspoon ground turmeric

4 cups (32 fl oz/1 L) coconut milk

2 cups (16 fl oz/500 ml) chicken or vegetable stock
(see pages 10 and 11)

salt and freshly ground black pepper, to taste

fresh tarragon leaves, for garnish

Heat vegetable oil in a large saucepan. Add chili pepper, garlic and ginger and stir-fry until aromatic, about 1 minute.

Add onions, carrots, cumin and turmeric and stir-fry until onions are softened, about 2 minutes.

Pour in coconut milk and stock. Bring to a boil, reduce heat to low and simmer, uncovered, until carrots are tender, 12–15 minutes. Remove from heat.

Transfer soup to a food processor or blender and process until smooth. Return soup to pan and heat through for 2 minutes.

Season with salt and pepper and serve, garnished with tarragon leaves.

Serves 4

Rustic potato soup with Thai spices

2 tablespoons olive oil

1 yellow (brown) onion, chopped

2 cloves garlic, chopped

1½ lb (625 g) potatoes, peeled and roughly chopped

2 tablespoons chopped cilantro (fresh coriander)

2 tablespoons chopped fresh flat-leaf (Italian) parsley

4 fresh kaffir lime leaves or 1 teaspoon grated lime zest

1 tablespoon peeled and grated fresh ginger

1 small red chili pepper, seeded and chopped

6 cups (48 fl oz/1.5 L) vegetable stock (see page 11)
    or water

salt and freshly ground black pepper, to taste

1½ cups (12 fl oz/375 ml) coconut milk

4 fresh kaffir lime leaves or 1 teaspoon grated lime zest,
    for garnish

Heat olive oil in a large saucepan over medium heat.
Add onion and garlic and cook until onion softens, about
2 minutes. Add potatoes, cilantro, parsley, lime leaves or
zest, ginger and chili pepper, and cook for 1 minute.

Add stock or water and bring to a boil. Reduce heat
to simmer, cover and cook until potatoes are tender,
20–25 minutes. Remove lime leaves and discard.

Break up some of the potatoes with a potato masher,
keeping texture of soup chunky. Season with salt and
pepper. Add coconut milk and heat through, about
2 minutes.

Serve warm, garnishing each portion with a lime leaf.

Serves 4

French onion soup

3 tablespoons butter

1 lb (500 g) onions, thinly sliced

1 cup (8 fl oz/250 ml) dry white wine

½ cup (4 fl oz/125 ml) water

5 cups (40 fl oz/1.25 L) chicken or beef stock
   (see pages 10 and 11)

salt and freshly ground black pepper, to taste

baguettes (French breadsticks), sliced and toasted,
   for serving

freshly grated gruyère cheese, for serving

Melt butter in a deep, heavy-based saucepan. Add onions, wine and water and cook very gently on low heat, stirring regularly, until onions are soft, 30–40 minutes. Add stock and season. Bring to a boil, cover, and simmer for 10 minutes.

Meanwhile, top toasted bread with grated cheese and broil (grill) until cheese is melted and golden.

Divide soup among individual bowls, and top each with a slice or two of bread. Serve immediately.

Serves 4–6

Variation

You can also place unmelted cheese and toast on top of the individual soup bowls and then pop the whole lot under the broiler (grill) so that the entire top is covered with cheese.

Mushroom-barley soup

2 tablespoons olive oil

1 leek, washed and thinly sliced, including some of
    light green portion

4 cloves garlic, crushed

2 sticks celery, diced

9 cups (72 fl oz/2.25 L) chicken or vegetable stock
    (see pages 10 and 11)

2 carrots, peeled and diced

¾ cup (4½ oz/140 g) pearl barley, rinsed

1 lb (500 g) white mushrooms, sliced

1 teaspoon salt, or to taste

½ teaspoon freshly ground black pepper, or to taste

In a large saucepan or soup pot, heat oil and sauté leek,
garlic and celery until translucent but not brown, about
10 minutes.

Add stock, carrots, barley and mushrooms and bring
to a boil. Reduce heat and simmer, stirring from time to
time, until barley is tender, about 2 hours. Add more
stock or water if soup becomes too thick.

Add salt and pepper and serve immediately.

Serves 8–10

Mushroom and cilantro soup

3 tablespoons light olive oil

1 yellow (brown) onion, chopped

2 cloves garlic, crushed

1 x 1 in (2.5 cm) piece fresh ginger, peeled and grated

5 cilantro (fresh coriander) roots, finely chopped

1 green chili pepper, finely chopped

3 tablespoons lime juice

3 cups (24 fl oz/750 ml) vegetable stock (see page 11)

3 cups (24 fl oz/750 ml) coconut milk

2 teaspoons fish sauce

1 lb (500 g) mixed mushrooms, sliced if large (see
    Hint page 116)

2 cups (2 oz/60 g) cilantro (fresh coriander) leaves

Heat 1 tablespoon oil in a large saucepan over
medium–high heat. Add onion, garlic, ginger, cilantro
roots and chili pepper and cook, stirring, until onion is
soft, about 5 minutes. Add lime juice, stock, coconut
milk and fish sauce and simmer for 15 minutes.

Meanwhile, heat remaining oil in a frying pan over
medium heat. Add mushrooms and cook, stirring, until
soft, about 5 minutes.

Reserve some mushroom slices for garnish. Add
remaining mushrooms and cilantro leaves to soup.
Working in batches, process soup in a food processor
until smooth, 1–2 minutes. Return soup to pan and
reheat over medium–high heat, about 2 minutes. Serve
immediately, garnished with reserved mushrooms.

Serves 4

RIGHT Mushroom and cilantro soup

Mushroom soup

1 teaspoon olive oil

1 slice bacon, most fat removed, finely chopped

3 scallions (shallots/spring onions), chopped

7 oz (220 g) mixed mushrooms, sliced if large (see Hint)

4 cups (32 fl oz/1 L) chicken stock (see page 10)

2 tablespoons chopped fresh parsley

salt and freshly ground black pepper, to taste

1 cup (2 oz/60 g) cooked small pasta

4 slices thick bread

4 slices gruyère cheese

Heat olive oil in a saucepan (preferably nonstick) over medium heat. Add bacon, scallions and mushrooms and cook, partially covered, for 5–10 minutes, stirring occasionally.

Add stock and bring to a boil. Stir in parsley, salt and pepper, and cooked pasta.

Top each slice of bread with a slice of cheese and broil (grill) until cheese melts. Serve immediately with hot soup.

Serves 2

Hint
Choose any type of mushroom or use a variety – oyster (abalone) mushrooms, wild mushrooms, large cultivated field mushrooms. Button mushrooms are just as delicious as any.

Red lentil soup

1½ cups (10 oz/300 g) dried red lentils

6 cups (48 fl oz/1.5 L) chicken or beef stock
(see pages 10 and 11) or water

1 yellow (brown) onion, grated

1 teaspoon ground cumin

salt and freshly ground black pepper, to taste

1 tablespoon lemon juice

olive oil, for serving

lemon wedges, for serving

FOR TOPPING

2 large yellow (brown) onions

¼ cup (2 fl oz/60 ml) olive oil

1–2 cloves garlic, finely chopped

Rinse lentils well in a sieve under cold running water.

Bring stock or water to a boil in a large soup pot. Add lentils and onion. Reduce heat to low, cover and simmer until lentils are tender, about 30 minutes. Do not stir during cooking. The lentils should have collapsed into a puree; for a finer texture, pass through a sieve or puree in a food processor.

Add cumin and season with salt and pepper. If a thinner soup is desired, add water. Stir in lemon juice and heat gently.

To make topping: Cut each onion in half lengthwise and thinly slice each half crosswise into semicircles. Heat olive oil in a frying pan over medium heat. Add onions and cook, stirring often, until golden brown, about 10 minutes. Add garlic, cook for a few seconds and remove from heat.

Serve the soup hot, in deep soup bowls, topping each serving with onion and garlic mixture. Offer extra olive oil to drizzle, and provide lemon wedges for squeezing into the soup.

Serves 6

Japanese watercress soup

6 cups (48 fl oz/1.5 L) chicken or vegetable stock
   (see pages 10 and 11)
2 tablespoons soy sauce
2 eggs
4 oz (125 g) watercress sprigs
white pepper, to taste
soy sauce, to taste (optional)

Heat stock and soy sauce in a large saucepan over medium–high heat. Bring liquid to a steady simmer. Simmer for 3–4 minutes. Increase heat to high and bring liquid to a boil.

In a small bowl, using a fork, lightly whisk eggs then stir into soup. Keep stirring until eggs are set. Soup must be boiling for eggs to set.

Reduce heat to medium–low and add watercress. Simmer until watercress is wilted, about 2 minutes.

Season with white pepper and soy sauce (if using), and serve immediately.

Serves 4

RIGHT Corn, pumpkin, spinach and rice soup

Corn, squash, rice and spinach soup

1 teaspoon sesame oil
2 tablespoons vegetable oil
1 medium yellow (brown) onion, chopped
1 x 2 in (5 cm) piece fresh ginger, peeled and
   finely chopped
6 ears of corn, kernels removed
10 oz (300 g) butternut squash (pumpkin), peeled and
   cut into chunks
¼ cup (2 oz/60 g) short- or medium-grain white rice
½ teaspoon salt
6 cups (48 fl oz/1.5 L) water
7 oz (220 g) cooked and drained spinach
pinch salt
sesame oil, to taste
chili paste or sambal oelek, for serving

Warm oils in a large pot over medium–high heat. Add onion and stir-fry until onion begins to color, about 2 minutes. Add ginger, corn kernels, butternut squash, rice and salt and stir-fry until mixture is coated with oil, about 1 minute. Add water and bring to a boil. Reduce heat and simmer, covered, until vegetables and rice are tender and beginning to break up, about 50 minutes. Leave soup as it is, or blend to a puree.

Reheat spinach in a steamer. Mix spinach with salt and a drizzle of sesame oil.

Pour soup into bowls, top with some spinach mixture and serve with chili paste or sambal oelek.

Serves 6–8

Chili-corn soup

3 tablespoons light olive oil

2 red chili peppers

1 medium yellow (brown) onion

2 cloves garlic, peeled

1 teaspoon dried shrimp paste (optional)

2 teaspoons finely grated lime zest (rind)

1 tablespoon chopped fresh ginger or fresh galangal or
   2 teaspoons galangal powder

1 tablespoon coriander seeds

1 teaspoon cumin seeds

½ teaspoon fennel seeds

½ teaspoon ground cardamom

8 cups (64 fl oz/2 L) chicken or vegetable stock
   (see pages 10 and 11)

4 cups (24 oz/750 g) fresh or frozen corn kernels

2 teaspoons fish sauce

1 tablespoon lime juice

1 roasted red bell pepper (capsicum), peeled and
   seeded

1 teaspoon chili paste or sambal oelek

Combine 2 tablespoons olive oil, chili peppers, onion, garlic, shrimp paste, lime zest, ginger and spices in a food processor and process to a smooth paste, 2–3 minutes.

Heat remaining oil in a large saucepan over medium heat and add paste. Cook, stirring, until fragrant, 3–4 minutes.

Add stock, increase heat to medium–high and bring liquid to a steady simmer. Add corn, fish sauce and lime juice and simmer until corn is tender, about 5 minutes. Let soup cool slightly.

Working in batches if necessary, ladle soup into a food processor and process until smooth, 2–3 minutes. Return soup to pan and reheat before serving.

In a food processor, process bell pepper and chili paste until smooth, about 2 minutes.

Ladle soup into individual bowls and garnish with bell pepper mixture.

Serves 4

Vegetable minestrone

5 oz (150 g) dried cannellini beans

3 cups (24 fl oz/750 ml) cold water

2 tablespoons olive oil

1 yellow (brown) onion, chopped

2 cloves garlic, crushed

1 potato, peeled and diced

2 carrots, peeled and diced

1 leek, trimmed and sliced

2 sticks celery, finely chopped

¼ small cabbage, finely shredded

8 cups (64 fl oz/2 L) vegetable stock (see page 11)

1 zucchini (courgette), sliced

2 tomatoes, peeled and chopped

4 oz (125 g) green beans, trimmed and cut into short lengths

4 oz (125 g) shelled peas

4 oz (125 g) pasta

2 tablespoons chopped fresh parsley

salt and freshly ground pepper, to taste

freshly grated parmesan cheese, for serving (optional)

Wash dried beans and place in a large bowl. Cover with cold water and leave to soak for at least 8 hours or overnight. Drain, rinse well and set aside.

Heat olive oil in a large, heavy-based saucepan and sauté onion and garlic until soft, about 5 minutes. Add drained cannellini beans, potato, carrots, celery, leek, cabbage and stock and bring to a boil. Cover and simmer until beans are tender, about 45 minutes.

Add zucchini, tomatoes, green beans, shelled peas and pasta and cook until pasta is cooked through, about 15 minutes.

Stir in parsley and season with salt and pepper. Serve hot, sprinkled with parmesan cheese, if using.

Serves 6–8

Sweet potato, carrot, ginger and tofu soup

2 tablespoons olive oil

1 medium yellow (brown) onion, chopped

14 oz (440 g) sweet potato, peeled and chopped

3 large carrots, peeled and chopped

3 teaspoons peeled and grated fresh ginger

2 small red chili peppers, seeded and finely chopped

1 tablespoon finely chopped cilantro (fresh coriander) stems

4 cups (32 fl oz/1 L) chicken stock (see page 10)

1 tablespoon soy sauce

10 oz (300 g) soft tofu, drained

salt and freshly ground black pepper, to taste

1 tablespoon finely chopped cilantro (fresh coriander) leaves, for garnish

FOR SOY AND LINSEED CROUTONS

4 slices soy and linseed bread

vegetable oil spray

To make soy and linseed croutons: Lightly spray both sides of bread with oil and place under a preheated broiler (grill). Broil (grill) until lightly browned, 2–3 minutes each side. Cut into triangles or strips.

In a large frying pan, heat olive oil over medium heat. Add onion, sweet potato and carrot and sauté, stirring occasionally, until softened but not browned, about 7–10 minutes. Add ginger, chili peppers, cilantro stems, stock and soy sauce and bring to a boil. Reduce heat and simmer for 15 minutes.

In a food processor, puree tofu and add gradually to soup. Puree soup in batches until smooth. Add salt and pepper.

Pour soup into bowls, garnish with cilantro and serve immediately with soy and linseed croutons.

Serves 4

Carrot soup with Asian greens and coconut

2 lb (1 kg) carrots, peeled and finely diced

1 large yellow (brown) onion, chopped

2 cloves garlic, chopped

6 cups (48 fl oz/1.5 L) chicken or vegetable stock
(see pages 10 and 11)

6½ oz (200 g) Asian greens such as bok choy or choy
sum, roughly sliced

juice of 1 lime

1 tablespoon chopped Thai basil leaves

4 tablespoons thick coconut cream, for serving

¼ cup (1 oz/30 g) unsweetened dried (desiccated)
shredded coconut, toasted, for garnish

Place carrots, onion, garlic and stock in a large
saucepan. Bring to a boil. Cover and cook until carrots
are soft, about 8 minutes.

Working in batches, puree soup in a food processor.
Return to pan and reheat over medium heat, about
5 minutes. Add greens, lime juice and basil and cook for
2 minutes.

Ladle into individual bowls and top each serving with
1 tablespoon coconut cream.

Serves 4

Mushroom wonton, noodle and spinach soup

9 oz (280 g) mixed oyster (abalone), shiitake and button
   mushrooms
½ teaspoon sea salt
½ teaspoon white pepper
3 tablespoons chopped cilantro (fresh coriander)
1 tablespoon peeled and grated fresh ginger
2 cloves garlic, roughly chopped
1 fresh or 2 dried kaffir lime leaves, finely chopped
   or 2 teaspoons finely grated lime zest
4 water chestnuts, finely chopped
1 small egg, lightly beaten
20 wonton wrappers
8 cups (64 fl oz/2 L) chicken or vegetable stock
   (see pages 10 and 11)
8 oz (250 g) fresh egg noodles
8 oz (250 g) baby English spinach leaves

Combine mushrooms, salt, pepper, cilantro, ginger, garlic
and kaffir lime leaf in a food processor and process until
smooth, about 2 minutes. Transfer mixture to a bowl and
stir in water chestnuts and egg.

Lay wonton wrappers on a dry surface and place
1 heaping teaspoon mushroom mixture in center of each
wrapper. Wet edges with a little water, using a pastry
brush or your finger, and fold edges in to form bundles,
pressing edges together to secure filling.

Place stock in a large saucepan over medium heat
and bring to a steady simmer.

Bring a large saucepan of water to a boil. Add
noodles and cook until tender, 5–7 minutes. Drain and
rinse noodles and add to stock.

Add wontons to stock and simmer until cooked
through, 5–6 minutes. Stir in spinach and cook until
wilted, 2–3 minutes.

Ladle soup into individual bowls and serve
immediately.

Serves 4

Butternut squash and coconut milk soup

12 oz (375 g) butternut squash (pumpkin), peeled and
   cut into 1 in (2.5 cm) pieces
2 tablespoons lime juice
1 large yellow (brown) onion, peeled and chopped
2 cloves garlic, chopped
1 x 2 in (5 cm) piece fresh ginger, peeled and chopped
3 red chili peppers
1 stalk lemongrass, bottom 3 in (7.5 cm) only,
   finely chopped

1 teaspoon dried shrimp paste
3 cups (24 fl oz/750 ml) coconut milk
1 cup (8 fl oz/250 ml) chicken or vegetable stock
   (see pages 10 and 11)
1 tablespoon fish sauce
½ cup (½ oz/15 g) baby basil leaves, for garnish

Place squash pieces in a large bowl and add lime juice.
Stir to combine and set aside.

Place onion, garlic, ginger, chili peppers, lemongrass
and shrimp paste in a food processor and process until
smooth, 2–3 minutes.

In a large saucepan, combine onion mixture with
¼ cup (2 fl oz/60 ml) coconut milk. Cook over
medium–high heat until mixture is fragrant and reduced,
about 5 minutes. Add remaining coconut milk, stock and
fish sauce and cook over medium–high heat, stirring,
until liquid begins to bubble. Simmer for 5 minutes.

Add squash pieces and lime juice and simmer until
squash is tender, 10–15 minutes.

Ladle soup into individual bowls and serve sprinkled
with basil leaves.

Serves 4

Chinese noodle soup

1 tablespoon vegetable oil

1 medium carrot, peeled and sliced into flowers

4 oz (125 g) bamboo shoot tips, julienned

10 dried shiitake mushrooms, soaked in hot water for
   30 minutes and drained

½ bunch (8 oz/250 g) choy sum (flowering cabbage)
   leaves, roughly chopped

3 scallions (shallots/ spring onions), trimmed and cut
   into 1 in (2.5 cm) pieces

1 oz (30 g) bean sprouts

1 teaspoon superfine (caster) sugar

½ teaspoon salt

1 tablespoon rice wine vinegar or sherry

2 tablespoons light soy sauce, plus extra for serving

10 oz (300 g) fresh flat egg noodles

8 cups (64 fl oz/2 L) vegetable stock, simmering
   (see page 11)

Heat vegetable oil in a wok over medium–high heat.
Stir-fry carrots, bamboo shoot tips and mushrooms for
3 minutes. Add choy sum, scallions and bean sprouts
and stir-fry for another minute. Stir in sugar, salt, rice
wine vinegar or sherry and light soy sauce.

Meanwhile, cook noodles in boiling water for
2 minutes. Drain, rinse in cold water and drain again.
Add cooked noodles to simmering stock and return
soup to a boil.

Stir in vegetables. Serve immediately, with extra soy
sauce to taste.

Serves 4–6

Vegetable and rice noodle soup (Buddha's delight)

4 oz (125 g) dried rice noodles

8 cups (64 fl oz/2 L) vegetable stock (see page 11)

2 cloves garlic, chopped

1 x 1 in (2.5 cm) piece fresh ginger, peeled and sliced

1 stalk lemongrass or zest of 1 lime, cut into
    1 in (2.5 cm) pieces

ground white pepper, to taste

1 tablespoon soy sauce, or to taste

1 tablespoon lime juice, or to taste

8 oz (250 g) butternut squash (pumpkin), cut into
    1 in (2.5 cm) cubes

4 oz (125 g) green beans

8 baby sweet corn cobs

1 carrot, peeled and julienned

1 bunch (13 oz/400 g) baby bok choy, leaves separated

1 green bell pepper (capsicum), seeded and sliced

4 oz (125 g) snow peas (mange-tout)

1 tomato, cut into 1 in (2.5 cm) cubes

2 sprigs fresh herbs, such as basil, cilantro (fresh
    coriander) or chives

4 sprigs fresh mint, for garnish

chili paste or sambal oelek, for serving

Bring a large saucepan of water to a boil and add noodles. Remove from heat and allow to stand until soft, 4–5 minutes. Drain, then divide noodles among individual bowls.

Place stock in a large saucepan over medium–high heat. Cover, and bring to a boil. Add garlic, ginger, lemongrass, white pepper, soy sauce and lime juice. Reduce heat to a simmer and cook for about 1 minute. Add squash, beans, corn and carrot and cook until tender–crisp, about 2 minutes. Add bok choy, bell pepper, snow peas, tomato and herbs and cook until vegetables are tender, about 3 minutes.

Ladle soup over noodles and garnish with mint. Serve immediately, with chili paste or sambal oelek.

Serves 4

Coconut and vegetable soup

1 tablespoon vegetable oil

¼ teaspoon shrimp paste

1 clove garlic, crushed

¼ cup (⅓ oz/10 g) chopped fresh cilantro (fresh coriander) stems

4 scallions (shallots/green onions), chopped

3 cups (24 fl oz/750 ml) chicken or vegetable stock (see pages 10 and 11)

1 cup (8 fl oz/250 ml) coconut milk

1 tablespoon fish sauce

6 oz (180 g) finely shredded green cabbage

12 snow peas (mange-touts), trimmed and sliced crosswise

1 carrot, peeled and julienned

3 oz (90 g) small broccoli florets

3 tablespoons lime juice

2 teaspoons chili paste or sambal oelek

1 tablespoon chopped cilantro (fresh coriander) leaves

In a wok, warm oil over medium heat. Add shrimp paste, garlic, cilantro stems and scallions and stir-fry until softened, about 1 minute. Add broth, coconut milk and fish sauce. Bring to a boil, then reduce heat to low.

Add cabbage, snow peas, carrot and broccoli. Simmer, uncovered, until vegetables are just tender, about 10 minutes.

Stir in lime juice, chili paste or sambal oelek and cilantro and serve immediately.

Serves 4

Vegetable pho

6 cups (48 fl oz/1.5 L) vegetable stock (see page 11)

6 cloves

4 black peppercorns

1 x 2 in (5 cm) piece fresh ginger, peeled and sliced

1 cinnamon stick

2 star anise

4 cardamom pods

1 tablespoon fish sauce

8 oz (250 g) green beans, sliced

8 oz (250 g) thick asparagus spears, cut into
    2 in (5 cm) pieces

8 oz (250 g) dried rice noodles

6 oz (180 g) chopped Asian greens, such as bok choy
    or choy sum, or baby English spinach

4 sprigs mint

4 sprigs cilantro (fresh coriander)

chili sauce, for serving

fish sauce, for serving

lime wedges, for serving

Combine stock, spices and fish sauce in a large saucepan over medium–high heat and bring to a steady simmer. Simmer until stock is infused with flavor, about 20 minutes. Strain through a fine sieve and discard solids. Return stock to pan and simmer gently over medium heat.

Bring a small saucepan of water to a boil. Add beans and asparagus and cook for 2 minutes. Drain, then set aside.

Place noodles in a bowl and cover with boiling water. Let stand until soft, about 5 minutes. Drain noodles and place in individual bowls. Top noodles with Chinese greens, cooked beans and asparagus, and mint and cilantro sprigs. Ladle stock into bowls.

Serve immediately, accompanied by chili sauce, fish sauce and lime wedges for diners to add according to taste.

Serves 4

Chilled soups

Gazpacho

1 x 13 oz (400 g) tomatoes, drained
1 cup (8 fl oz/250 ml) tomato juice
2 teaspoons balsamic or white wine vinegar
1 tablespoon olive oil
½ red bell pepper (capsicum), seeded and
  finely chopped
½ small red onion, finely chopped
1 small cucumber, finely diced
7 oz (220 g) cooked shrimp (prawns), peeled
  and chopped
1 tablespoon chopped fresh parsley
½ small avocado, peeled and diced

Combine tomatoes, tomato juice, vinegar and oil in a
food processor and puree until smooth. Chill for at least
20 minutes.

Stir in remaining ingredients and serve.

Serves 2

Cold apricot and pear soup

⅔ cup (4 oz/125 g) dried apricots
⅔ cup (4 oz/125 g) dried pears
⅔ cup (4 oz/125 g) prunes, pitted
3 cups (24 fl oz/750 ml) cold water
¼ cup (2 oz/60 g) sugar
1 cup (8 fl oz/250 ml) dry white wine
2 red apples, peeled, cored and chopped
1 cinnamon stick
1 tablespoon fresh lemon juice
6 teaspoons plain (natural) low-fat yogurt

Wash dried fruit in warm water. In a bowl, combine fruit,
water and sugar. Refrigerate overnight.

In a saucepan, cook fruit and soaking water, wine,
apple and cinnamon stick until very soft, about
20 minutes. Remove cinnamon stick and puree mixture
in a food processor. Stir in lemon juice. Refrigerate for at
least 2 hours.

Serve in bowls, topped with 1 teaspoon yogurt.

Serves 6

RIGHT Gazpacho

Cold avocado soup

2 avocados, halved, with seeds removed
1 small white onion, chopped
2 cups (16 fl oz/500 ml) chicken stock (see page 10)
1 cup (8 fl oz/250 ml) buttermilk
salt and freshly ground black pepper, to taste
1 red bell pepper (capsicum), halved
1 teaspoon Tabasco sauce

Scrape avocado flesh into a food processor. Add onion and stock and process until smooth. Pour soup into a bowl and stir in buttermilk and salt and pepper. Set aside until ready to serve.

Put bell pepper under a broiler (grill) until the skin blackens. Transfer to a plastic bag and leave for about 30 minutes. Scrape off the blackened skin. Put bell pepper and Tabasco sauce in a food processor and puree until smooth.

Just before serving, add a dollop of bell pepper puree to each bowl of avocado soup.

Serves 4

Asparagus and dill soup

1 leek
6 tablespoons oil
½ teaspoon salt
15 asparagus spears
4 cups (32 fl oz/1 L) chicken stock (see page 10)
fresh dill, chopped, for serving
plain (natural) yogurt or heavy (double) cream,
   for serving (optional)

Cut off most, but not all, of the green part of the leek, then make two cross cuts almost to the root. Rinse well in a sink full of water. Chop finely.

Heat oil in a heavy-based saucepan and add leek and salt. Stir, then cover and cook gently until leek softens, stirring occasionally.

Break the tough end off each asparagus spear and discard, then finely slice stalks, but not tips. Set tips aside. Add sliced stalks to leek and stir through. Continue cooking until asparagus starts to soften, about 5 minutes.

Transfer mixture to a food processor, add a little stock and puree.

Return puree to pan with remaining stock and asparagus tips, and bring gently to a simmer, stirring occasionally.

Just before serving, stir through a generous amount of fresh dill. Add a dollop of good quality yogurt or cream to individual bowls if using.

Serves 4

Hint
This soup can also be served hot—simply reheat just before serving.

Chilled cucumber and ginger soup

12 small English (hothouse) cucumbers, peeled and
    seeded
3 teaspoons sea salt
2 teaspoons peeled and grated fresh ginger
freshly ground black pepper, to taste
¾ cup (6 oz/180 g) plain (natural) yogurt
1 small English (hothouse) cucumber, peeled, seeded
    and sliced, for garnish
dill sprigs, for garnish

Slice cucumbers in half lengthwise. Sprinkle with
2 teaspoons sea salt, place in a colander and allow to
stand for 30 minutes. Rinse cucumbers well under cold
water. Roughly chop and place in a food processor. Add
ginger, remaining salt and pepper, and process until
mixture forms a thick puree, about 20 seconds.

Transfer 1 cup (8 oz/250 g) puree to a bowl. Cover
and refrigerate. Firmly press remaining puree through a
fine sieve to produce a clear, cucumber-flavored liquid.
Discard solids. Cover and refrigerate cucumber liquid.
Refrigerate puree and liquid for 1 hour.

Place ¼ cup (2 oz/60 g) cucumber puree in the
center of each serving bowl. Pour cucumber liquid
around pulp. Top each serving with 2 tablespoons
yogurt. Garnish with cucumber slices and dill sprigs.
Serves 3–4

Roasted red bell pepper soup

6 large red bell peppers (capsicums)
8–10 plum (Roma) tomatoes, peeled, seeded and
    chopped
1 tablespoon olive oil
2–4 cloves garlic, finely chopped
3 cups (24 fl oz/750 ml) chicken stock (see page 10)
salt and freshly ground black pepper, to taste
whole fresh basil leaves, for garnish
finely sliced lemon, for garnish

Cut bell peppers in half through stem and remove seeds and white membrane. Place cut side down onto parchment-lined (baking paper lined) baking sheets and bake at 425°F (220°C/Gas 7) or broil (grill) until skin is blistered and charred, about 15 minutes.

Place charred peppers in a plastic bag. Seal and allow to stand for 15 minutes. Remove peppers from bags then peel away and discard skins.

Place three of the peppers with tomatoes in a food processor and puree until smooth. Slice remaining pepper into strips and set aside.

Place olive oil in a saucepan over low heat. Add garlic and cook until fragrant, about 2 minutes. Add pepper puree and stock, bring to a boil and simmer for 15 minutes. Season to taste with salt and pepper. Allow to cool.

Refrigerate until ready to serve, then ladle into bowls and garnish with whole basil leaves and a slice of lemon.

Serves 4

Vichysoisse

3 tablespoons butter
3 large leeks, trimmed of most green and finely sliced
1 onion, thinly sliced
1 lb (500 g) potatoes, peeled and diced
3¾ cups (30 fl oz/900 ml) chicken or vegetable stock
    (see pages 10 and 11)
salt and ground white pepper, to taste
¼ teaspoon ground coriander
1 egg yolk
⅔ cup (5 fl oz/150 ml) light (single) cream
snipped fresh chives, for garnish

Melt butter in a large saucepan and sauté leek and onion very gently for about 5 minutes, without browning. Add potato, stock, seasonings and cilantro and bring to a boil. Cover and simmer gently until vegetables are very tender, about 30 minutes.

Cool a little, then sieve or puree soup in a food processor and pour into a clean saucepan.

Blend egg yolk with cream and whisk evenly into the soup. Reheat gently, without boiling. Adjust seasonings, cool, then chill thoroughly.

Serve sprinkled liberally with snipped chives.

Serves 6

Hint

This classic dish can also be served hot – simply reheat just before serving.

Glossary

ANCHOVIES, DRIED (IKAN BILIS) Salted preserved fish, available from Asian food stores. Substitute anchovy paste, available in supermarkets.

ARROWROOT A useful ingredient for thickening soups. Cornstarch (cornflour) may be substituted.

ASIAN CHILI OIL Vegetable oil infused with chilies and often tinged red, available from Asian food stores.

ASIAN SESAME OIL A nutty-tasting, fragrant and richly colored oil made from toasted, crushed sesame seeds and available from Asian food stores. Only small amounts are required for flavoring.

BEAN SPROUTS Sprouted green mung beans sold fresh or canned. Fresh sprouts have a crisper texture and a more delicate flavor. Store in the refrigerator for up to 3 days.

BUTTERMILK Made commercially from nonfat or lowfat milk and fortified with milk solids, to which a benign culture of acid-producing bacteria has been added. Buttermilk has a pleasant, light tang and a thick, creamy consistency.

CANNELLINI BEANS Large, elongated kidney-shaped beans, creamy white in color, traditionally used in soups and salads. Also known as white kidney beans.

CARDOMOM Whole green pods filled with fragrant, tiny black seeds. For best flavor, grind the seeds just before using. Also available as pre-ground cardamom seeds.

CANDLENUTS Hard oily nuts available at Asian food stores. Macadamia nuts or almonds may be substituted.

CHERVIL A ferny-leaved herb that resembles parsley and tastes like aniseed. Store up to 1 week in a plastic bag in the refrigerator.

CHORIZO A spiced, coarsely textured cured sausage, originally from Spain. Made from pork, pork fat, garlic and paprika.

CHILI PEPPERS As a general rule, the smaller the chili, the hotter it is. For a milder taste, remove the seeds and membrane. Dried chili pepper flakes and chili powder may be substituted.

CHINESE CELERY Darker green and stronger in flavor than regular celery, which may be substituted.

CHINESE CHIVES, FLAT OR GARLIC Flat-leaved chives with a distinct garlic odor. Substitute standard chives or scallions (shallots/spring onions).

CHINESE ROAST DUCK Sold in Chinese markets or barbecue stores, usually displayed hanging in the window. Store for up to 2 days in the refrigerator.

CILANTRO (CORIANDER) Pungent, fragrant leaves from the coriander plant, resembling parsley. The roots of the plant are often used to flavor Asian-style soups.

CINNAMON STICKS Rolled and layered pieces of bark from the cinnamon tree. Both the sticks and ground form are readily available.

COCONUT MILK/CREAM Made by pressing freshly grated coconut and widely available in cans. Avoid buying sweetened coconut milk or "cream of coconut."

CORIANDER SEEDS Usually dry-roasted in a frying pan before being ground. Freshly ground coriander seeds have a fragrance that is both lemony and herbaceous.

CLOVES Dried buds of a tree that grows in Southeast Asia and the West Indies, with a sharp but sweet flavor.

CRÈME FRAÎCHE A cultured cream product with a tangy, tart flavor, similar to sour cream in texture. Substitute sour cream if unavailable.

CUMIN SEEDS From a plant in the parsley family. Briefly dry-roasting brings out their flavor, which is earthy, pungent and a little bitter. Use whole or ground.

DAIKON Japanese giant white radish, at least 20 inches (50 cm) long. Less pungent than many other radishes and contains various enzymes to aid digestion.

DAEPA Resemble scallions (shallots/spring onions) in flavor but lack the onion aroma. Substitute scallions.

DASHI, INSTANT A Japanese stock, also available as granules from Asian food stores.

FENNEL SEEDS From the fennel plant, used whole or ground, to impart an aniseed-like flavor.

FENUGREEK SEEDS From the fenugreek plant. Briefly dry-roasting brings out their bitter, sharp and nutty flavor. Use whole or ground.

FISH SAUCE Made from the fermented extract of salted small fish. Used both as a table condiment and in the kitchen in Thai and Vietnamese cuisine. Can be stored in the refrigerator for up to 6 months.

FLAT-LEAF (ITALIAN) PARSLEY Parsley with a flat leaf and a stronger flavor than curly parsley. Store for up to 1 week in the refrigerator.

GALANGAL A pink rhizome related to ginger. Used fresh in soups or in curry pastes. Fresh ginger may be substituted. Some recipes also call for powdered galangal.

GARLIC Fresh garlic ensures better flavor than pastes, dried flakes or the pre-crushed version sold in jars. The smaller the garlic bulbs, the stronger the flavor.

GINGER A thick rootlike rhizome of the ginger plant. Store fresh ginger in the refrigerator for 2–3 days.

GRUYÈRE A firm to hard cow's cheese from Switzerland, nutty yet earthy in character. Swiss-style cheese may be substituted.

HOT BEAN PASTE A spicy, thick red-brown sauce made from fermented soybeans, chilies, garlic and spices. Available from Asian food stores, it is sometimes called hot red bean paste or chili bean paste.

KAFFIR LIME LEAVES Fragrant leaves commonly added to Asian soups or pounded into curry pastes. If fresh leaves are unavailable, use frozen or dried.

LEMONGRASS A herb commonly used in Asian soups. Remove the outer leaves and bruise or chop finely.

MATCHA A green-tea powder used to make a bitter, caffeine-rich form of tea customarily drunk in Japan.

LENTILS Green/brown lentils have a slightly nutty flavor and hold their shape when cooked. Red lentils are smaller with a mild, slightly sweet flavor and become mushy when cooked.

MISO PASTE A thick paste of fermented ground soybeans, used in Japanese soups. May be kept refrigerated for up to 1 year.

MUSHROOMS Chinese dried or shiitake mushrooms are sold in packets at Asian food stores. Soak in hot water and remove tough stems before using. Shiitake are also available fresh at good supermarkets and Asian food stores. Enoki mushrooms are pale with long thin stalks topped by tiny caps, have a mild flavor and crunchy texture. Creamy white oyster mushrooms have large, soft, fan-shaped caps and a very mild, delicate flavor. Straw mushrooms have a closed-umbrella top and are sold canned or dried, and occasionally fresh.

NOODLES Egg noodles are available in a variety of widths, thin, round or flat, and fresh or dried. Hokkien are thick, round yellow noodles, readily available fresh in the refrigerated section of most supermarkets. Ramen are Japanese egg noodles available dried from Asian food stores. Rice stick noodles or vermicelli are made from ground rice and water, and are widely available dried or fresh in a vast array of sizes and textures, all commonly added to Asian-style soups. Somen are traditional Japanese soup noodles made from wheat flour and oil. Available fresh or dried in an array of colors. Udon are soft, creamy white Japanese noodles made from wheat flour dough, available fresh or dried.

NUTMEG Dried nutmeg, a seed, is available whole or ground.

PALM SUGAR Made from palm trees and available soft in bottles or hard in blocks which must be shaved before using. Substitute firmly packed light brown sugar.

PARMESAN A hard, strong-tasting cheese used as a topping and a flavoring. Grate just before using.

RICE VINEGAR A mild vinegar fermented from rice and especially popular in Asia. Low in acidity.

RICE WINE Also known as shaoxing, rice wine is made from sticky (glutinous) rice. Substitute dry sherry.

SAMBAL OELEK A spicy Indonesian paste made from ground chilies, salt and sometimes vinegar and sold in jars. It can be used instead of fresh chilies. Refrigerate after opening.

SCALLION Also known as shallot or spring onion. An immature onion with little or no bulb and long, straight green leaves.

SEAWEED, DRIED A coldwater seaweed, also known as kombu, available from Asian supermarkets. Wipe with a damp cloth before use.

SESAME SEEDS Seeds of an herb that grows in India and other parts of Asia. Whole or ground white sesame seeds are used in many Asian dishes. The seeds may be toasted to enhance their flavor.

SHALLOT (FRENCH SHALLOT) A small, hard clove-shaped onion with reddish-brown skin. Packaged deep fried shallots are available at Asian food stores (see page 92).

SHRIMP, DRIED Available unrefrigerated at Asian food stores, these strong-tasting shrimp make a quick base for soup. Omit if unavailable.

SHRIMP PASTE, DRIED A pungent, darkly colored hard paste made from fermented shrimp, available unrefrigerated at Asian food stores. Once open, it should be sealed tightly. Omit if unavailable.

SOYBEAN PASTE Made from fermented soy beans. Used in cooking, not as a table condiment, it is available in Thai, Chinese and Korean varieties. See also Hot Bean Paste.

SOY SAUCE Made from soybeans and used in cooking soups and as a table condiment. Available in light and dark varieties. Use soy sauce within 1 month of opening, or keep refrigerated for up to 6 months.

STAR ANISE Dried fruit from a variety of evergreen magnolia tree. Identifiable by its eight-arched pods, it has a similar flavor to aniseed.

TEMPEH A cake of fermented, cooked soybeans with a mild nutty flavor and a texture similar to meat. Readily available in refrigerated vacuum-sealed packets.

THAI RED CURRY PASTE A ready-made paste made from Asian ingredients and spices. Available from Asian food stores and supermarkets.

TOFU Available in refrigerated vacuum-sealed packs and shelf-stable cartons in supermarkets in firm, soft and silken styles which may be added to soups in cubes or blended as a base. Deep fried tofu may be used as a garnish in laksas.

TURMERIC, GROUND A bright yellow spice widely used to add both color and flavor to soups.

WAKAME A highly nutritious seaweed, available dried or salted. Used in Japanese soups.

WASABI Very hot, Japanese green horseradish, traditionally served with sushi and sashimi. Available ready to use in tubes or in powdered form.

WONTON WRAPPERS Available fresh or frozen in a variety of colors and shapes. Fresh wrappers will keep for up to 7 days in the refrigerator, or they may be frozen.

Index

apricot and pear soup, cold, 132
Asian greens, carrot soup and coconut with, 124
asparagus
   asparagus and dill soup, 135
   beef soup with ginger and asparagus, 58
   crab and asparagus soup, 89
   pork wonton asparagus and noodle soup, 70
avocado soup, cold, 134

barley
   beef and barley soup, 55
   mushroom-barley soup, 114
beans
   peasant bean soup, 105
   poached salmon and green bean soup, 86
   spicy squash and bean soup, 19
beef
   beef and barley soup, 55
   beef and cabbage soup, 56
   beef soup with ginger and asparagus, 58
   beef with coconut milk and Thai herbs, 60
   beef stock, 11
   borscht, 55
   classic beef pho, 50
   marinated beef laksa, 59
   meatball soup, 53
   pho beef stock, 11
   quick beef and pepper soup, 52
beet
   and potato borscht, creamy, 19
   borscht, 55
bell pepper
   quick beef and pepper soup, 52
   roasted red bell pepper soup, 137
bisque, shrimp, 75
borscht, 19, 55
bouillabaisse, 80

broccoli soup (cream of), 29
Buddha's delight, 128

cabbage
   beef and cabbage soup 56
capsicum see bell pepper
caldo verde see spinach
carrot
   carrot and ginger soup, 110
   carrot soup with Asian greens and coconut, 124
   sweet potato, carrot, ginger and tofu soup, 123
cauliflower
   curried cauliflower soup, 102
   Du Barry soup, 30
   potato and cauliflower soup, 30
   spicy tomato and cauliflower soup, 102
chicken
   chicken and coconut milk soup, 37
   chicken and mushroom soup, 34
   chicken and noodle soup, 45
   chicken and sweet corn soup, 39
   chicken laksa, 32
   chicken soup, 42
   chicken stock, 10
   chicken vermicelli soup with egg, 38
   hot and sour chicken soup, 43
   sweet potato chowder with chicken, 35
   Vietnamese chicken and rice soup, 40
chili
   chili-corn soup, 120
   marinated lime-and-chili fish soup, 97
   shrimp, tomato and chili soup, 76
   sweet potato, chili and coconut soup, 101
Chinese barbecue pork, 71
Chinese roast duck see roast duck
chorizo, spicy corn and tomato soup with, 63

chowder
   clam, 82
   sweet potato chowder with chicken, 35
clam chowder, 82
coconut
   carrot soup with Asian greens and coconut, 124
   coconut and vegetable soup, 130
   coconut-shrimp soup, 91
   sweet potato, chili and coconut soup, 101
   beef with coconut milk and Thai herbs, 60
   butternut squash and coconut milk soup, 126
   chicken and coconut milk soup, 37
   mussels in spiced coconut milk broth, 78
corn
   chicken and sweet corn soup, 39
   chili-corn soup, 120
   corn, squash, rice and spinach soup, 118
   spicy corn and tomato soup with chorizo, 63
crab
   crab and asparagus soup, 89
   sour crabmeat soup, 90
cucumber and ginger soup, chilled, 136
curried cauliflower soup, 102
curried parsnip soup with parsnip chips, 16
curried split pea soup, 23

Du Barry soup, 30
duck see roast duck

egg, chicken vermicelli soup with, 38

fennel and oyster soup, 84
fish
   fish stock, 12
   Indian fish soup, 78
   marinated lime-and-chili fish soup, 97

gazpacho, 132
ginger
   beef soup with ginger and asparagus, 58
   carrot and ginger soup, 110
   chilled cucumber and ginger soup, 136
   miso with tuna and ginger, 94
   sweet potato, carrot, ginger and tofu soup, 123

ham
   red lentil, potato and ham soup, 67
   smoked ham minestrone, 66
   split pea and ham soup, 64
hazelnuts, steamed squash soup with, 24

laksa
   chicken, 32
   marinated beef, 59
   paste, 13
   seafood, 92
leek
   creamy squash and leek soup, 23
   pea, potato, leek and tofu soup, 101
   scallop and leek soup, 85
lentil
   spinach and lentil soup, 106
   vegetable and lentil soup, 108
lettuce soup, pea and, 27

meatball soup, 53
minestrone
   smoked ham, 66
   vegetable, 121
miso
   basic miso soup, 15
   miso with tuna and ginger, 94
mushroom
   chicken and mushroom soup, 34
   mushroom and cilantro soup, 114
   mushroom-barley soup, 114
   mushroom soup, 116
   mushroom wonton, noodle and spinach soup, 125

udon noodle soup with sesame pork and mushroom, 69
mussels in spiced coconut milk broth, 78

noodle
  chicken and noodle soup, 45
  Chinese noodle soup, 127
  marinated shrimp, noodle and herb soup, 95
  mushroom wonton, noodle and spinach soup, 125
  pork wonton asparagus and noodle soup, 70
  ramen noodle and roast duck soup, 46
  somen noodle, pork and scallion soup, 71
  udon noodle soup with sesame pork and mushroom, 69
  vegetable and rice noodle soup, 128

onion
  French onion soup, 113
  shrimp and onion soup, 76
oyster
  fennel and oyster soup, 84

parsnip soup, curried, with parsnip chips, 16
pasta, country vegetable soup with, 105
pea
  pea and lettuce soup, 27
  pea, potato, leek and tofu soup, 101
pho
  classic beef, 50
  stock, 11
  vegetable, 131
pork
  pork wonton asparagus and noodle soup, 70
  somen noodle, pork and scallion soup, 71
  udon noodle soup with sesame pork and mushroom, 69
potato
  creamed squash and potato soup, 20

creamy beet and potato borscht, 19
  Du Barry soup, 30
  hearty potato and salami soup, 62
  pea, potato, leek and tofu soup, 101
  potato and cauliflower soup, 30
  potato and watercress soup, 20
  red lentil, potato and ham soup, 67
  rustic potato soup with Thai spices, 112
  scallop and potato soup, 85
prawn see shrimp
pumpkin see squash

ramen noodle and roast duck soup, 46
red lentil
  red lentil, potato and ham soup, 67
  red lentil soup, 117
rice
  corn, squash, rice and spinach soup, 118
  salmon rice soup, 72
  Vietnamese chicken and rice soup, 40
roast duck
  ramen noodle and roast duck soup, 46
  roast duck and sweet potato soup, 49

salami soup, hearty potato and, 62
salmon
  poached salmon and green bean soup, 86
  salmon rice soup, 72
scallop
  scallop and leek soup, 85
  scallop and potato soup, 85
seafood
  quick seafood stock, 12
  seafood laksa, 92
  seafood soup, 81
shrimp
  coconut-shrimp soup, 91

hot and sour shrimp soup, 76
  marinated shrimp, noodle and herb soup, 95
  shrimp and onion soup, 76
  shrimp bisque, 75
  shrimp, tomato and chili soup, 76
somen noodle, pork and scallion soup, 71
spinach
  caldo verde, 29
  corn, squash, rice and spinach soup, 118
  cream of spinach soup, 26
  mushroom wonton, noodle and spinach soup, 125
  spinach and lentil soup, 106
  spinach soup, 29
split pea
  curried split pea soup, 23
  split pea and ham soup, 64
squash
  butternut squash and coconut milk soup, 126
  corn, squash, rice and spinach soup, 118
  creamed squash and potato soup, 20
  creamy squash and leek soup, 23
  spicy squash and bean soup, 19
  steamed squash soup with hazelnuts, 24
stock
  beef, 11
  chicken, 10
  fish, 12
  hot and sour, 13
  pho beef, 11
  quick seafood, 12
  vegetable, 11
sweet corn see corn
sweet potato
  roast duck and sweet potato soup, 49
  sweet potato, carrot, ginger and tofu soup, 123
  sweet potato, chili and coconut soup, 101
  sweet potato chowder with chicken, 35

Thai herbs
  beef with coconut milk and Thai herbs, 60
  vichysoisse with Thai herbs, 109
Thai spices, rustic potato soup with, 112
tofu
  pea, potato, leek and tofu soup, 101
  sweet potato, carrot, ginger and tofu soup, 123
  tofu and vegetable soup, 98
tomato
  cream of tomato soup, 21
  shrimp, tomato and chili soup, 76
  spicy corn and tomato soup with chorizo, 63
  spicy tomato and cauliflower soup, 102
  tomato soup, 106
tuna, miso with ginger and, 94

udon noodle soup with sesame pork and mushroom, 69

vegetable
  chunky vegetable soup, 104
  coconut and vegetable soup, 130
  country vegetable soup with pasta, 105
  tofu and vegetable soup, 98
  vegetable and lentil soup, 108
  vegetable and rice noodle soup, 128
  vegetable minestrone, 121
  vegetable pho, 131
  vegetable stock, 11
vermicelli
  chicken vermicelli soup with egg, 38
vichysoisse, 137
  Thai herbs, with, 109

watercress
  Japanese watercress soup, 118
  potato and watercress soup, 20

Weights and measurements

The conversions given in the recipes in this book are approximate. Whichever system you use, remember to follow it consistently, to ensure that the proportions are consistent throughout a recipe.

Weights

Imperial	Metric
1/3 oz	10 g
1/2 oz	15 g
3/4 oz	20 g
1 oz	30 g
2 oz	60 g
3 oz	90 g
4 oz (1/4 lb)	125 g
5 oz (1/3 lb)	150 g
6 oz	180 g
7 oz	220 g
8 oz (1/2 lb)	250 g
9 oz	280 g
10 oz	300 g
11 oz	330 g
12 oz (3/4 lb)	375 g
16 oz (1 lb)	500 g
2 lb	1 kg
3 lb	1.5 kg
4 lb	2 kg

Volume

Imperial	Metric	Cup
1 fl oz	30 ml	
2 fl oz	60 ml	1/4
3 fl oz	90 ml	1/3
4 fl oz	125 ml	1/2
5 fl oz	150 ml	2/3
6 fl oz	180 ml	3/4
8 fl oz	250 ml	1
10 fl oz	300 ml	1 1/4
12 fl oz	375 ml	1 1/2
13 fl oz	400 ml	1 2/3
14 fl oz	440 ml	1 3/4
16 fl oz	500 ml	2
24 fl oz	750 ml	3
32 fl oz	1 L	4

Oven temperature guide

The Celsius (°C) and Fahrenheit (°F) temperatures in this chart apply to most electric ovens. Decrease by 25°F or 10°C for a gas oven or refer to the manufacturer's temperature guide. For temperatures below 325°F (160°C), do not decrease the given temperature.

Oven description	°C	°F	Gas Mark
Cool	110	225	1/4
	130	250	1/2
Very slow	140	275	1
	150	300	2
Slow	170	325	3
Moderate	180	350	4
	190	375	5
Moderately hot	200	400	6
Fairly hot	220	425	7
Hot	230	450	8
Very hot	240	475	9
Extremely hot	250	500	10

Useful conversions

1/4 teaspoon	1.25 ml
1/2 teaspoon	2.5 ml
1 teaspoon	5 ml
1 Australian tablespoon	20 ml (4 teaspoons)
1 UK/US tablespoon	15 ml (3 teaspoons)

Butter/Shortening

1 tablespoon	1/2 oz	15 g
1 1/2 tablespoons	3/4 oz	20 g
2 tablespoons	1 oz	30 g
3 tablespoons	1 1/2 oz	45 g